to mom with love
a son's story

to mom with love
a son's story

DENNIS R. PIANA

TATE PUBLISHING & *Enterprises*

To Mom With Love...A Son's Story
Copyright © 2010 by Dennis R. Piana. All rights reserved.

No part of this publication may be reproduced, stored in a retrieval system or transmitted in any way by any means, electronic, mechanical, photocopy, recording or otherwise without the prior permission of the author except as provided by USA copyright law.

The opinions expressed by the author are not necessarily those of Tate Publishing, LLC.

Published by Tate Publishing & Enterprises, LLC
127 E. Trade Center Terrace | Mustang, Oklahoma 73064 USA
1.888.361.9473 | www.tatepublishing.com

Tate Publishing is committed to excellence in the publishing industry. The company reflects the philosophy established by the founders, based on Psalm 68:11,
"The Lord gave the word and great was the company of those who published it."

Book design copyright © 2010 by Tate Publishing, LLC. All rights reserved.
Cover design by Kellie Southerland
Interior design by Scott Parrish

Published in the United States of America

ISBN: 978-1-61663-589-3
1. Biography & Autobiography, Women
10.06.07

It's all about caring. The ultimate tribute.

Dedication

To my wife, Hennie, "Uno Cosa Bene Del Dio"—a gift of God, whose love, sacrifice, and devotion gave me the support and help I needed to carry on.

Introduction

ASK NOT WHAT YOUR PARENTS CAN DO FOR YOU...
ASK WHAT YOU CAN DO FOR YOUR PARENTS.

In our fast-paced society of high technology and dual-career families, the art of raising children is becoming more and more the responsibility of daycare centers and nannies. The high cost of living and the wants and needs of individuals leave no time for them to be caregivers to children, let alone an aging parent. Today's senior citizens have been left to survive on their own in assisted living facilities or nursing homes by the "Me" generation; all-too-often forgotten, and only remembered when the inheritance is due. The "baby boomers" and "pre-baby boomers" are now faced with the reality of raising a family, helping support grandchildren, and assisting aged parents. This is often financially and emotionally overwhelming and burdensome.

When push comes to shove, usually the aged parents are left out in the cold to fend for themselves. Their once active and productive years are now wrought with idleness and a sense of not belonging. Society, as well as family, has shifted their focus to the young. The elderly feel unwanted and often in the way. Their isolation is overlooked and only they know the pain of loneliness. There is an old saying: One mother can take care of ten children, but ten children cannot take care of one mother. Sad but true!

This story is about an extraordinary woman who cared for and gave so much love to others her whole life, and a son who was able to, in turn, respect, love, and care for her in her final years. It's about the beauty and joy of giving; it's about respect and duty; it's about love and inner peace. This story takes you on a journey to where we all someday arrive.

Chapter 1

And then there was Louise…

To be able to fully understand and appreciate this incredibly talented and loving woman, I have to fill you in on some of her background. So let's start at the beginning.

Louise was born in Brooklyn, New York, on September 18, 1907, to immigrants from Naples, Italy. She grew up in the back of her father's barbershop along with her mother and younger sister. On the next two upper floors of the building were her two aunts and two uncles, who had no children, and a widowed grandmother. In the surrounding neighborhood were all her parents' relatives and friends from the old country. Her parents' friends became her friends and their children became her playmates. The streets and brownstone stoops were their playground. It wasn't always playtime for Louise; children in those days were given adult responsibilities because everyone from the old country worked out of necessity—the American dream. Her mother worked in a garment factory, and as early as nine years old, Louise would come home from school and prepare the evening dinners under the watchful eye of her grandmother. She would do all the grocery shopping at the local markets and barter with the local merchants in Italian and English. The pasta was handmade and the sauce was from scratch.

Weekends were full of family gatherings and food. All the relatives and old world friends in the neighborhood would congregate at Louise's. It wasn't uncommon to have as many as twenty people for dinner. As was universal in the Italian household, each and every Sunday meal was a banquet—replete with soups, salads, pasta, meat, and of course homemade pastries. Louise would be cooking side by side with her mother and aunts while the men reminisced about the labors of the week or told tales of the old country. The food was simple but plentiful and always accompanied by wine. From the age of ten, Louise was taught to accompany her food with two small glasses of homemade wine.

Her father loved opera music and would often sing arias from his favorite operas while shaving or working in his barbershop. He would often tear-up while singing; something Louise always admired about her father was his sensitivity and love for music. She grew up listening to her father singing and it wasn't long before she would sing along with him. She loved the musical part of opera and showed an interest in learning how to play the piano; so the next step was her introduction to the piano. Her parents hired an old German professor of music who was from the old school—strict and demanding. Hour upon hour she would practice the classical instructions under his authoritarian supervision. It became a long and grueling learning process—long lessons and countless hours of practice. Louise displayed a remarkable ability in grasping how to read sheet music and an unusual agility with her fingers on the piano keys. She loved classical music, but there was something inside her that wanted to be able to play the popular tunes of her era—more lively and trendy. Louise would hide the modern sheet music she bought under her piano bench and when no one was around, she would practice all the new hit songs. Her piano instructor had forbid her to play anything but classical music, but in her effort to be popular, she continued to sneak in music that was more contemporary. Suddenly, those family gatherings were not only about food, but it was a day of music and dance. Oh yes, she did entertain the older relatives with classical and opera tunes; but then she would liven it up with all the songs that were new and trendy. She had all the cousins dancing and swinging until the evening hours—most of whom she taught how to dance.

Life then was not always about food and song; it had its serious side and sad side as well. Louise, being fluent in Italian and English, was often the interpreter for the family. She would accompany the entire family to doctor appointments, deal with lawyers and business merchants, handle all the mail, and reconcile neighborhood and family arguments. When Louise was twelve, her grandmother passed away, and as was customary in those days, the body was waked in the home. Relatives and friends would visit the family and pay their respects while the body was on view in the parlor. Louise would help prepare food for the visitors and it was her job to escort the children to view her grandmother. She learned at an early age how to arrange funeral and burial services for family members, which in subsequent years became an ever too frequent task. Louise seemed to have a stoic strength and calm about her, a maturity beyond her years; and yet, she maintained a healthy and positive outlook on life.

Holidays were always celebrated in a big way—abundant food and wine and special homemade "dolce" sweets. These meals were not the plain everyday pastas or meats; they were elaborate assortments of the finest and choicest ingredients. The preparation phase took hours and days—a tradition that is still carried out in the Italian household today. The most special of these holidays was the Christmas Eve dinner, "la Vigila"—the vigil. This special dinner was the most difficult and elaborate of all the holiday feasts. It was a meatless meal consisting of a variety of fresh fish as well as other Italian pasta specialties. Louise would learn that Christmas was not about receiving gifts but about the gift of giving to your family a special feast from your heart. This gift has been handed down for generations and is now part of my special gift to my family. There were many other holidays and occasions that were celebrated with spectacular meals of plenty. The other ingredient that was added to these feasts were plenty of family and friends; and to show everyone how special they were, Louise's father would finish off the meal by serving his guests "the drink of kings," Liquore Strega. This was an after-dinner cordial from the Benevento region of Italy from which they immigrated.

The art of entertaining would become one of Louise's specialties as the years progressed. Her family, relatives, and friends would always look forward to sharing a Sunday dinner or holiday meal prepared by Louise. Over the years, she fine-tuned and elaborated on all the old world traditional dishes. She would create meals that were truly a culinary experience and, oh yes, culminated with a glass of Strega!

Louise displayed many other talents in her early years in addition to cooking and music. Her mother, being a seamstress in the garment industry, was always sewing or hemming an article of clothing during the evening hours. Louise would watch her mother with fascination as she stitched and mended articles of clothing for the family. She would often fall asleep listening to the humming of the sewing machine motor. Her mother taught Louise how to thread a needle, sew a hem, and cut material. It wasn't long before Louise would be sewing for the family. She was very artistic and would often draw a sketch of a dress or redesign a pre-existing garment. The whole neighborhood soon learned of her skills as a seamstress. She would alter waistlines, shorten sleeves, and redo the hemlines for all the local women.

When Louise was fifteen years old, one of her close girlfriends from the neighborhood, who was about to graduate high school, asked her to accompany her to Pratt Institute where she wanted to apply for enrollment. She felt Louise would be able to help her with the application process. Louise always appeared older than she was—she was tall and always carried herself in a sophisticated manner. The receptionist in the admissions office, thinking that Louise was there also to apply, handed both girls enrollment applications. Louise and her girlfriend filled out the applications and handed them in. Three weeks later, Louise received an acceptance in the mail from Pratt Institute; by the way, her girlfriend was not accepted. It wasn't uncommon in those days to apply for higher education without transcripts or high school diplomas. So, at the age of fifteen, Louise entered Pratt Institute as a fashion design major.

It wasn't long before the instructors recognized Louise's special talents and her attention to detail. She finished projects ahead of schedule and was given extra courses to fill her time. Louise amazed the faculty with her ideas and designs, and accelerated through the curriculum in record time. While she was a student, Louise was asked by several families to design dresses and gowns for them. She made wedding dresses, prom gowns, formal wear, and party dresses. They supplied the material and Louise supplied the talent.

The final exam before graduation consisted of a three-day project in the auditorium—each student was to design a dress, make the pattern, cut the material, drape the mannequin, and present the final product for evaluation and grading. The regular faculty and two outside professional designers conducted the grading. Louise proceeded through the test with methodical detail and precision swiftness. At one point, she noticed one of the examiners, a professional designer, watching her every move. In her self-assured manner, she asked him, "Can I help you?" He just motioned to her to continue what she was doing. At the conclusion of the exam, the examiners gathered and followed the professional designer to where Louise was standing. He announced to the faculty and students that Louise's design and final product would be used as the basis for passing.

At the age of seventeen, Louise graduated Pratt Institute. That summer, Mr. Bergdorf, who was the professional designer during the exam, hired her as an assistant designer for Bergdorf Goodman. Little did she know that this was a stepping-stone to a long and rewarding career. At first, her duties as an assistant designer were minimal—most of the senior designers felt threatened by her youth and obvious abilities. As time passed, they grew to realize that she was a talent to be reckoned with; her ideas, designs, and innovations caught their attention and she was soon given her own design room. Her lunch hours were spent at the Plaza Hotel in Manhattan, not to eat lunch, but to sit at a table and observe the high society women from abroad as they moved about the hotel. Louise would focus in on a particular part of a dress being worn by the socialites, taking note of anything new or innovative, and then she would sketch what she saw. She would return to her design room and develop a full-scale drawing of a dress incorporating what she found interesting that afternoon. Needless to say, the styles from Italy and France were soon to be expanded upon by the American fashion industry. Louise had a knack for zooming in on something and duplicating or enhancing it, whether it was a neckline, a sleeve design, or a hemline. This talent was soon noticed by her superiors—so off to Paris she went at the age of nineteen.

In a strict Italian household, the idea of a nineteen-year-old girl traveling to Europe by herself was unheard of in the early 1920s. Her parents were eager to help her career, knowing that this was an opportunity of a lifetime. The only way that she would be permitted to travel to Europe was with a chaperone. Louise and her mother sailed for Paris in the spring of 1927. It was a fashion designer's dream come true. She was to spend three months in Paris attending fashion shows and gala affairs, with the objective of keeping her eyes wide open. Little did she know that she would witness history in the making. After an arduous nine-day voyage, she and her mother arrived in Paris. Upon their disembarking, Louise noticed American flags flying everywhere—draped on buildings and hanging from windows and flagpoles. She asked her mother why all those flags were flying. Her mother answered, "I hope you don't think they are for you!" No, they were not for Louise—they were for Charles Lindbergh, the American flyer who was expected to land at any moment after completing the first transatlantic flight from New York to Paris, an historic event which captured the attention of the whole world and changed the course of aviation history.

Louise and her mother went to the landing field outside Paris to witness Lindbergh's arrival amidst thousands of flag-waving spectators. They waited in the damp and dimly lit airfield for hours; waiting and looking into the starlit sky for any signs of a plane. After what seemed to be an eternity, the droning of the engine of Lindbergh's plane broke the silent vigil. The crowd immediately exploded into screams and cheers as the plane descended from the sky. The crowds burst through the barricades and rushed the plane as it landed. Louise was able to see him as he was lifted out of the plane. A memory forever in her mind; a story forever told!

The celebrations surrounding Lindbergh's flight lasted for a few days with parades and street parties. Louise, so impressed with all the festivities, documented every moment in her diary, which, seventy-five years later, would prove to be *her* moment in history.

For the next three months, Louise attended fashion shows and visited designer fashion houses throughout Paris. The rules were strict when in attendance at these events—no sketchpads or photographic equipment. Louise, after sitting for hours and watching the assortment of designs, would leave the showrooms and immediately return to her hotel room and frantically sketch what she had seen on the fashion runways. She would spend countless hours until the early dawn recreating all the new designs. It wasn't all work; there were many social functions that she and her mother attended. They frequented the coffee shops, went to the theater, and took long strolls in the evening along the gas-lit streets of Paris. While sitting in outdoor cafés, Louise's eyes were always focused on the women as they walked in the streets, hoping to catch a glimpse of a new design. She always had a sketchpad or napkin handy in the event she saw something that caught her eye. By the time Louise and her mother left Paris, she had a portfolio of every garment that would soon be on the streets and in showrooms around the world. Without a doubt, it was a tremendous value to the American fashion industry and a catapulting event in Louise's career.

Upon her return, family and friends, as well as colleagues, greeted her. Italians celebrate everything in a big way! She attended dinner parties and house parties, recounting her journey and her special moments—and of course, wearing the latest Parisian designer dresses. She soon became a storyteller and historian of pre-war Paris. Adults and children alike listened to her escapades with wide-eyed and open-mouthed attention. Louise's popularity mounted, and before she knew it, she was entered in a beauty contest held in New York by the barbers association. Yes, Louise was crowned queen, and enjoyed all the accolades and gifts that came with being a queen. And of course, she made the gown that she wore for the contest!

Louise soon became the head designer at a large fashion house in Manhattan, commanding an entourage of assistant designers. Known now as "Miss Louise," she drew the attention of all the design houses in New York. Buyers, designers, and fashion houses were knocking at her door, offering her all sorts of financial incentives to design for them. Her code of ethics and loyalty kept her right where she was. She was content and happy with her position and her employer. Her wants and lifestyle were simple—after all, she was a simple girl from Brooklyn, still living at home with her parents. Her only extravagance was the opera. During the opera season at the Metropolitan Opera, she would treat her mother and father to dinner and an evening at the opera on a weekly basis. Her joy was seeing her father's tears during each performance.

Louise's strength and sense of duty to family was once again challenged. Her mother's cousin was killed by a trolley car one rainy night. He was the sole support of his wife and two sons, one of whom had just started at New York University. There was no income to pay for rent and food, let alone college, so her cousin, Tony, decided to leave college and seek employment to support his mother and brother. Louise, not wanting her cousin to leave college, arranged for the family to move in with her and her family. There was always room for family in her parents' home. Sacrifice and giving came easy for Louise, especially since she was financially successful and family-oriented. Her cousin, Tony, continued his college studies and his family was able to carry on.

Tony later graduated NYU and embarked on a career in teaching, later achieving the distinction of becoming the Dean of St. John's University in New York.

Good times and happy families soon turned to tragedy: the Depression of 1929. Louise's career was still intact, but she saw the way things were going: businesses going under, bankers and businessmen selling apples on the street, and people jumping out of windows after losing fortunes. She witnessed the long food lines, the long unemployment lines, and the long, sad faces. After a year of witnessing the hardships families and associates encountered, and enduring the ever-sinking economy, Louise made a decision that would alter her life and career forever. Since there was insecurity in the business world, she decided to leave the fashion designing industry and become a fashion design teacher. She felt there was security in being a teacher in New York City.

Louise, not knowing the procedures or qualifications needed to secure a teacher's license, scheduled an interview with the chancellor's office at the Board of Education. She presented her resume and credentials to Mr. Ritter, the presiding chancellor at that time. After reviewing Louise's documents, he had one comment. "Are you crazy, young lady?" He was referring to the fact that as a designer, she was earning $200 per week and as a substitute teacher, she would earn $6 per day. He informed her that in order for her to obtain a substitute-teaching license, she would have to go back to school and take the basic education courses required by New York State. Undaunted by the chancellor's comments, Louise enrolled in Oswego State Teacher's College in the summer of 1931. Having tackled so many challenges in the past, Louise adapted to her new role as student easily. Once again, she was able to dazzle her instructors with her skills and her eagerness to succeed. She completed one year of course work during an accelerated three month summer session. She returned home with her basic requirements in hand and scheduled another appointment with the Board of Education.

Louise received her substitute-teaching license in the fall of 1931. She knew all too well that she had to hone her skills as a teacher and complete other courses in education in order to obtain a full-time teaching license. She enrolled in night courses during that year and taught at the local high school in Brooklyn on a per diem basis. Her steadfast determination and fearless drive once again lead her to a final goal: a new career as an educator, entrusted with the responsibility of shaping minds and passing on a myriad of skills.

Chapter 2

Louise Finds Love…

Louise quickly adapted to her new role as a teacher. She loved the interaction with students and found their enthusiasm and quest for knowledge inspiring. Learning fashion design was more interesting and fun than learning history or English. The students were able to work with their hands and see a final project. There were some technical aspects to the course, such as learning the content of different fabrics, the mechanics of stitching, and the art of drawing and converting that sketch into a pattern. Louise's experience in the design industry put her one notch above the other teachers in her field. The other teachers only had training in design from technical schools, and they all lacked industry experience. Louise, on the other hand, lacked the formal educational background in teaching. She knew she had to continue her studies at night in order to earn the credentials necessary to be appointed as a full-time teacher.

Still living at home, Louise was expected to do all the household chores as before. She continued her cooking and entertaining for the family. Her part-time teaching, evening classes, and household responsibilities left no time for a social life outside the home. She was popular with all the boys because she could play the piano and dance, but she always found them too young and immature. One would speculate that she was too mature and much too serious for her age. Louise never had any dating or romantic experiences as a young girl growing up—she was always involved with family matters, school, and work. She was always focused, deeply committed, and conscientious in whatever she did. For her, it was all work and no play. Others admired her strength and determination. To Louise, her work was her passion; whatever she did, she did with enthusiasm, confidence, never hesitant, and never deviating from her objective.

Continuing her education with the objective of obtaining a full-time teaching license spurred Louise on once again—a new goal sought after with the same determination and commitment as all her previous endeavors. She knew where she was going and what it took to get there. Whatever she tackled, she gave it her all—a trait that hallmarked her entire life. Her coursework at night was not too difficult and she enjoyed her teachers and admired their dedication to their profession. Since Louise was older than most of the students and had a more mature and sophisticated manner about her, she was often asked to supervise the class when a teacher was absent for any reason. One such occasion arose one evening when a teacher from another class needed someone to administer an examination to his class while he attended a college function. Louise willingly accepted the opportunity to fill in and add to her experience as a teacher. She never anticipated that this opportunity would change her life forever with a brief encounter that would lead to a deeply committed and enduring relationship.

Never having met the teacher she was to substitute for, and not knowing what was expected of her, made Louise feel a little uncomfortable. When she arrived at the classroom that evening, she found written instructions outlining her assignment. She was to hand out the examination booklets, sit at the desk to monitor the students, and at the end of the period, collect the completed tests. Louise was a little disappointed with the assignment, feeling that it was not a real teaching role, but nonetheless she carried out the assignment as instructed. During the examination, she was able to work on some of her own studies, so not all was wasted. At the end of the examination, she collected the tests from the students, put the booklets in the desk drawer, and left for the evening. The next evening, her teacher gave her a note from the teacher for whom she substituted the previous evening, requesting that she meet him at the end of her class. Not knowing what to expect, possibly another assignment or just a simple thank you, Louise promptly went to meet the teacher.

Upon arriving outside the classroom, Louise noticed a group of students gathered around the teacher—mostly young women—smiling and laughing. She waited in the doorway, not wanting to interrupt the gathering. She noticed the teacher, a handsome young man, smiling and joking with his students. Something about him gave Louise the impression that he was somewhat of a Casanova. A few moments passed and the teacher looked in her direction and said, "Can I help you, young lady?" Louise entered the room with style and grace, well-poised and confident, and handed the teacher the note she had received earlier. He dismissed the group of students and gave his undivided attention to Louise. He introduced himself as Salvatore, and thanked her for substituting the evening before. After exchanging introductions, they proceeded to casually discuss teaching, briefly touching on each other's background and educational experiences. The conversation was light and cordial. Sal, as he preferred to be called, asked Louise if he could accompany her to the bus stop since it was the end of evening classes. Louise and Sal left the building, quietly walking, sometimes engaging in short and somewhat strained conversation. Louise sensed that Sal had more on his mind than a casual walk to the bus stop. She felt a little uncomfortable and uneasy—after all, she was not used to male companions and flirtatious talk.

The walks to the bus stop became a routine, sometimes interrupted by a visit to the local soda shop on the way. The conversations ultimately led both Sal and Louise to come to the realization that there was a commonalty in their aspirations and their heritage, as well as their experiences in the fashion industry. Sal was born on July 7, 1907, in Catania, Sicily, the southern region of Italy, and immigrated to the United States at the age of three. His father, who died in a tragic accident at a young age, owned and operated a coat and suit manufacturing factory in the garment center where Sal had learned to be a tailor. He, too, was continuing his education in anticipation of being appointed to a full-time teaching position. He had graduated from NYU and was working on his master's degree in foreign languages.

Even though they were both of Italian origin, there was a difference—a huge difference in those days amongst Italians. Sal was Sicilian and Louise was Neapolitan. A diverseness equal to the War Between the States—the North and the South; a rivalry identical to that between the New York Yankees and the Brooklyn Dodgers! Louise realized that, as the relationship developed, there would be a time when Sal would meet her family: North meeting South. Feelings of trepidation filled her mind, wondering what her parents would think. She had become very fond of Sal and wanted so much for her family to like him. Louise spoke to her parents, telling them that she has met a fine young Italian man, and that she would very much like them to meet him. Her parents agreed to meet the young man. Sal arrived at Louise's home one Saturday evening to call on her and meet her parents. He was greeted at the door by Louise's younger sister, Peggy, and escorted to the front parlor. He was met in the parlor by Louise, who promptly introduced him to her parents, who were sitting on the sofa. Cordialities were exchanged and then Sal sat in a parlor chair next to Louise and her sister. Sal was the first to break the silence with a complimentary remark, in Italian, about the décor of the parlor. Louise's parents were immediately impressed with Sal's ability to speak the pure Tuscan form of Italian—an easy task for Sal since he was a foreign language teacher. He had the ability to speak French, Italian, Spanish, and English with such fluency that one would think he was a native from the region of the language he was speaking. The family encounter went well—it was short and sweet. Sal and Louise quickly exited and went on their date to the local movie theatre.

    It took some time before Louise's parents found out that Sal was Sicilian. It wasn't as traumatic for the family as Louise thought it might have been. They liked the young man; he was intelligent, good looking, and they knew he was in love with their daughter. The Sicilian "thing," to them, was a minor issue! Sal and Louise continued their courtship, consisting of movie dates, college dances, and family dinners. Sal's family and Louise's family eventually met each other; one would speculate that the Sicilian and Neapolitan "thing" never became an issue. The two families respected each other and got along for the sake of their children, recognizing and accepting the fact that they were in love.

Louise and Sal were married on June 4, 1934. Relatives and friends from both sides of the family attended—the Sicilians on one side of the banquet hall and the Neapolitans on the other. Past rivalries and differences were put aside once the music started playing and the wine stated flowing. It wasn't long before both sides were hugging and kissing, singing and dancing, and eating and drinking. Italians have a proclivity for making an ordinary celebration turn into a feast. This was no ordinary celebration; Louise and Sal were the first to marry in the new country, sparking a new era in their lives filled with joy and hope for the new Americans and their offspring. The weddings back in the old country were simple and down-to-earth, but here in America they were transformed into an elaborate extravaganza. Champagne toasts, five course dinners, desserts, coffee, wedding cake, and of course the Viennese table replete with fine pastries and liquors—and of course, Strega!

After spending a brief honeymoon in Niagara Falls and Québec, Canada, Louise and Sal returned to New York to begin their life together. They moved into an apartment, which they shared with Sal's widowed mother and younger brother, Ray, who was also a struggling, young, part-time teacher. Not the ideal way to start out married life as a young couple. Louise knew that Sal had to help support his mother, and as his wife, she too shared that responsibility. Obligation and sacrifice were commonplace then, and Sal knew that Louise was the perfect wife to handle the responsibility. Louise was accustomed to cooking and caring for family, something she had done since she was a child; now she had the added responsibility of a new family. Yes, Louise still took care of family matters for her parents and her aunts and uncles. Louise's father had developed diabetes, and it was her job every morning, before going to work, to go to her parents' house and administer her father's insulin injection and make sure he had the proper diet—a new role as nurse and dietician. Modern medicine was new to the immigrants from the old world and it took a lot to convince them of its benefits. They soon learned there were other remedies besides wine and garlic!

Louise and Sal struggled through their part-time teaching, schooling, family responsibilities, and a somewhat limited social life. The honeymoon was definitely over—now on to the real world, filled with hard work, sacrifice, and mounting responsibilities. Nothing came easy; it was only hard work and dedication that led to success, something that was typical of that generation. Louise completed her required courses and was appointed as a full-time teacher in the local high school. Her field of fashion design was very much in demand in the high schools in New York, while Sal's specialty, foreign languages, was not in demand. Sal finished his master's degree and continued his studies toward his doctorate. Louise contributed most of the income to the family, while Sal worked part-time as a substitute teacher and part-time tutor. A full-time teacher was not paid a high salary, but it was a steady and secure profession, which was exactly what Louise wanted.

Louise and Sal had both wanted to start a family of their own, but they knew it would be impossible due to their family obligations and financial situation. They continued on with their lives, hoping that someday they would both be full-time teachers, and one day have a family and home of their own. To own a home and raise a family in America—the American dream sought after by their ancestors! The lingering years of the Great Depression made that dream more difficult for most people, yet they endured and sacrificed in anticipation that soon all their dreams and aspirations would be realized. Like most other newly married couples of their generation, Louise and Sal tried to save what little they could so they could realize that dream. The everyday expenses left very little for extravagances, let alone savings. Vacations and dining in restaurants were out of the question; the local movie and a trip to the soda shop was an evening out. Everyone feared for their job security in those days and the expression of "saving for a rainy day" was of paramount importance.

Sal's brother Ray was appointed as a full-time teacher of chemistry in the local high school and was able to contribute more to the financial coffers of the family. Having lived in tight quarters and with a lack of privacy for two years, Louise felt it was time for her and Sal to start their own household—a nest of their own where they could feel free to develop their relationship unencumbered by family interference. Ray was not pleased with the idea of them moving out and leaving him to take care of his mother all by himself. He disagreed with Louise's need for privacy and felt that she was being selfish and immature. Louise stuck to her guns and convinced Sal that their marriage needed a breath of fresh air—a new beginning. Sal, reluctant at first, ultimately gave in to Louise; they moved into a one-bedroom apartment a few blocks away. It was a small apartment, but they were finally on their own. Louise did not abandon her mother-in-law and brother-in-law; quite the contrary, she shopped for them and prepared most of their evening meals. Louise also continued taking care of her father, whose health was deteriorating rapidly.

Louise's weekdays were full, to say the least; however, she and Sal found time on the weekends to be on their own and relax. Saturday's relaxation was usually centered around a sporting event, since Sal was an outstanding athlete and avid sports fan. They went to Yankee baseball games and NYU football games, sometimes traveling to out of town games. Relaxing on Sunday for Louise was having the family over for dinner. She kept both the families together—aunts, uncles, cousins, and old world as well as new world friends. She was the cohesive bond; the ultimate homemaker and entertainer. Life continued on, the economy improving and relationships expanding; all seemed well. Louise's sister, Peggy, met and fell in love with a young medical doctor, Lou, who was in his second year of residency. The families were jubilant as the courtship progressed and wedding plans were in the making. Oh yes, Louise was to design and make her sister's wedding gown.

The joy surrounding the impending marriage was tragically interrupted by the sudden death of Louise's father. His death threw the entire family into shock—the man so loved and respected by all was taken from them. Louise was affected the most by his passing, but once again her strength and resolve was needed to help the family through this heartbreaking time. She led them through the painful ordeal of the funeral services, ever vigilant of their frail emotions, while keeping her own pain concealed. She knew she had to be the Gibraltar of the family, a role too often taken, yet assumed with willingness and strength. Louise arranged the funeral services for her father, which consisted of a two-day wake in a Brooklyn funeral parlor, a high mass at the local church, and the burial at St. John's cemetery. The custom of using funeral parlors was new to Louise and her family; while sparing them the ritual of an in-home wake, it hastened the emptiness of the house and the feeling of separation. It lacked the warmth and comfort of their home, leaving them uneasy and isolated. No matter what the venue, saying good-bye to a loved one is never painless.

Peggy and Lou were married shortly after. Their wedding was small and intimate; no gala affair, no extravagant banquet, just a small gathering of the immediate family shrouded under a cloud of sadness.

They had to carry on with their lives, as did the rest of the family. Moving forward, putting sorrow behind them, and focusing on the future, they moved into a small apartment near Queens General Hospital while Lou finished his residency in urology.

In time, all the feelings of sorrow and emptiness seemed to fade and the routines of everyday life consumed most of their energy. After working diligently side by side and sacrificing, Louise and Sal finally realized their dream of owning a home. In 1938 they, with some financial help from Louise's mother, moved into a newly built home in Flushing, Queens—a new up and coming area in suburban New York. It was a three-bedroom brick and stucco, Tudor-style home situated on a 40x100 foot lot. To them it was a spacious palace, complete with eat-in kitchen, formal dinning room and living room, and a large back yard. A piece of America, a sanctuary for generations to come! The family gatherings and dinners continued, utilizing all the space in their new home—the kitchen full of women cooking, the dinning room full of Italian delicacies, and the living room full of men recanting their weeklong labors. Louise was able to expand her entertaining skills in her new home with pride and confidence. Louise and Sal loved their new home and all that it meant to them—it was their palace and Louise was the queen! Now, in her home, she made her guests feel like royalty by serving them *Strega* as her father had done in his.

Sal's brother Ray was the next to marry, and once again, it was time for the North and South to meet and celebrate a young couple's love—yes, his new bride was also a Neapolitan. As per usual, it was a gala affair—an enduring tradition now well-tolerated and established in New York. Ray and his bride, Frances, went on a brief honeymoon and returned to the apartment that he shared with his mother; once again, not the ideal situation. Ray, now realizing he needed some time with his bride to adjust to their new relationship, went to Louise for help. He asked her if she and Sal would have his mother move in with them in their new house since they had more than ample room to accommodate her. Louise, knowing all too well their need for privacy, gladly granted him his request. Ray, now realizing how Louise had felt four years prior, was repentant for his lack of understanding. Louise, as gracious as always, welcomed her mother-in-law into her home, and treated her with the respect expected from a dutiful daughter-in-law. Caring for people, especially family, came naturally to Louise; it was also how she was brought up—having had her elderly grandmother around growing up. Louise made her mother-in-law feel special by preparing her favorite Sicilian foods, which in turn also pleased her husband. Louise had a knack for knowing exactly what made people happy. After four months, Sal's mother missed her old neighborhood and longed to be back in her familiar surroundings with her old friends and younger son. Ray, sensitive to his mother's needs, brought her back to live with him and his wife.

Lou finished his residency training and was offered an opportunity to open a practice in a small growing city tucked away in the fertile green mountains of Vermont. The local hospital did not have an urologist on its staff, making his practice critical to that region of the state. Peggy was reluctant to leave New York and her family, but she realized she had to support her husband's career decisions. Moving on July 4, 1939, was certainly not Peggy's idea of celebrating Independence Day; it was more like being cast into the wilderness. Rutland, Vermont, with a population of 12,000 people, was hardly the metropolis Peggy was accustomed to, especially after living in New York City her entire life. She missed the excitement and the sophisticated way of life of New York, the enormity of its shopping, and its electrifying nightlife; but most of all, she missed her family. It took numerous phone calls and constant encouragement from Louise to convince Peggy that there was a rich and rewarding future on the horizon. It was a difficult adjustment, but Peggy soon surmounted the hurdles of the long cold and dank winters of New England and the feelings of separation and isolation from family. In time, she grew to love the serenity and peacefulness of her surroundings; a hamlet nestled in the beautiful countryside and bounded by majestic mountains.

Chapter 3

AND NOW IT'S A FAMILY...

Louise continued to immerse herself in her role as teacher and homemaker, while Sal dredged on, trying to get a full-time position in the school system. It was disappointment after disappointment for Sal, as foreign languages were not yet in vogue; he became more and more despondent and discouraged. Louise kept assuring him that his field would soon be accepted in the high schools in New York. Feeling confident, she encouraged him to continue his doctoral studies. Her income and steady position was adequate to support them and maintain the household while he studied; after all, what could get in their way? God has a way of giving you pleasant surprises at an inopportune time. Yes, Louise became pregnant. Their joy and excitement overshadowed their feelings of trepidation as they began to realize their new role as expectant parents. An event to culminate the American dream: a life, a home, and a family in America!

Louise couldn't wait to share her good news with her family and friends. She immediately called her sister in Vermont to tell her of her pregnancy, when Peggy, also excited, informed Louise that she too was pregnant; both expecting in the same month. Both sisters shared in their excitement and reveled in their joy. The rest of the family was jubilant over the coming event. Louise, while happy about her condition, was somewhat frightened about her ability to continue teaching and being the major financial contributor to the household. She knew at some point that she would have to leave school and lose her salary. Sal was also concerned, since he was not appointed yet to a full-time position and his income was sporadic and insufficient to raise a family. Sal began to take on more part-time teaching and tutoring jobs, working day and night and on weekends. As the months progressed, Louise began to tire and weaken; her feet began to swell from standing in the classroom for hours on end. She knew it would not be long before she would have to stop teaching.

Even though the board of education allowed teachers to take a maternity leave and return to teaching once the child was born, Louise was concerned about how her child would be cared for if she were to return to work. She knew they could not afford a babysitter or full-time nanny, and daycare centers were not available to families in those days. She could not give up teaching and become a full-time mother and homemaker without jeopardizing their financial stability. Now in the final months of her pregnancy, panic started to creep in and dampen the joy of the birth of their first child.

For the previous two years, since Louise's father died, her mother had been living alone, maintaining her own household and enjoying a somewhat comfortable retirement. She missed having her daughters in her home, but she was resigned to the fact that they were on their own and starting their own families. Her sisters and brothers were close by and they spent a lot of time together. As a concerned mother, she was worried about Louise's feelings of insecurity and uncertainty. She knew how hard Louise had worked to establish her career and the sacrifices she had endured. A mother's love knows no bounds; she knew her place was with her daughter. Once again, a family united for a common goal! She informed Louise and Sal that she was willing to give up her home and familiar surroundings, move in with them, and help raise their baby once it was born. This would allow Louise to return to teaching and provide a safe and loving environment for the baby. Having a grandmother in the home was familiar and comfortable to Louise. She knew the benefits that a nurturing relationship of a grandparent would have on her child—a treasured relationship of love, learning, and respect. Louise and Sal were relieved, knowing that their lives would soon be back on the road to security.

Louise was able to finish the school term at the end of June and prepare herself for the birth of her child in August. It became more and more difficult for Louise to stand and take care of the house and cook meals. Her mother moved in to help her during those final months. She took over all the household duties, allowing Louise more time to stay off her feet and rest. Louise enjoyed having her mother with her; it gave her a sense of security and comfort. They were always close and were used to taking care of each other; it was a familiar and warm relationship. Her mother was excited about her soon-to-be new role in the family: grandmother, a place of distinction and respect in a family. She would be the "Nanny," a cute and loving title for a grandmother. Nanny would be a caregiver, a teacher, a counselor, and a respected figure in the home. A trusted part of the family, who would have a place in the home, help provide stability and love to a growing family, and in turn, receive love and have a feeling of being needed and wanted: a sense of belonging, something everyone craves.

Louise's delivery date was rapidly approaching, and the excitement and anticipation was mounting. Sal was still working day and night, but managed to stay in close contact in order to be ready for the trip to the hospital. Louise would be the first in her family to deliver a baby in a hospital setting. When Louise was born, it was customary for births to take place in the home with either a midwife or doctor assisting in the delivery. Nanny kept a close eye on Louise, making sure that when the moment arrived, everything would go smoothly. Every day was a vigil, looking for signs that Louise was ready. The whole family, relatives and friends, were eagerly waiting for Louise to give birth—the first to create the new American generation. Since Sal was a naturalized American and Louise was born from naturalized American parents, this child would be the first American of Italian descent to be born to parents married in America—the new Americans!

On August 6, 1940, Louise gave birth to a beautiful and healthy baby boy. Both Louise and Sal were overjoyed and thrilled with the birth of their new son, Anthony Joseph—Anthony in memory of Sal's late father and Joseph for Louise's father. All the relatives and friends came to the hospital to view baby Anthony in the nursery. Sal beamed with pride and joy as Louise cuddled their newborn treasure: the new American, a son to carry on the dream and carry on the family name. Suddenly, all the uncertainty and fears left Sal and Louise; all they could think of was their precious son and their hopes and aspirations for him. Their thoughts and dreams were centered on Anthony's welfare and future. Now their lives would take on a new meaning; it was not just about husband and wife, it was a new family with new dreams and new direction. All the love and caring that they were capable of was bestowed upon their son. No sacrifice or hardship would be too great for them to endure when it came to Anthony. After five days, Louise brought her baby home from the hospital. Her mother and an entourage of loving aunts and uncles greeted her. Anthony was the center of attention, captivating the minds and hearts of all the relatives. Nanny looked at Louise with tears of joy, remembering when she herself gave birth—the feeling of completeness and contentment.

Three weeks later, Louise's sister, Peggy, gave birth to a beautiful baby girl, whom they called Johanna. Once again, the family reveled with delight over the birth of a new baby into the family. Peggy felt a little saddened over the fact that her family was not able to be with her when she gave birth, but she understood it was difficult for her relatives to travel so far. She was filled with pride over having given birth to a beautiful baby girl. Both she and Lou were thrilled beyond joy; they were so anxious to show off their little princess to their families. Louise arranged to have the christening of both their babies at the same time in New York. Peggy and Lou, along with Johanna, drove down from Vermont for the dual christening. Both sisters hugged and cried tears of joy over their new children. Anthony and Johanna were placed side by side in matching bassinettes on display for the whole family to admire. The house was full and the sound of babies crying echoed off the walls; it was a cacophony of shrills and squeals that lasted for hours. The two cousins made their tiny presence known in a big way by serenading their parents throughout the night. Louise and Peggy took turns throughout the night rocking and cradling the babies to sleep. It was a marathon; when one stopped crying and fell to sleep, the other would start in and wake the one who was sleeping. The zombie mothers paced the floor all night long.

Since Holy Family Parish had not yet completed construction of their church, Anthony and Johanna were to be christened in a tent that acted as a temporary church. Louise had made the christening garments for both babies—they looked like two cherubs dressed for a special presentation to God. The crying of the two young opera singers drowned out the solemnity of the Catholic sacrament of baptism; once again, each trying to out-perform the other. Having survived the ceremony, the family went back to Louise and Sal's house for a celebration dinner. Yes, it was an Italian feast commensurate for the momentous occasion—they toasted to the good health of the babies with *Strega!*

Anthony became the center of attention for the family in New York as all the family gatherings once again were at Louise's home. It was a constant procession of friends and relatives coming for dinner and sharing in Anthony's growth. He was the entertainment center and Louise was the host. Everyone enjoyed his happy and cheerful disposition; he knew he was on stage and he always gave them a show filled with amusement and laughter. He was a beautiful baby with fine, chiseled features, dark, piercing eyes, and a smile that mesmerized your senses. After a full day of merriment, Anthony was bombarded with goodnight hugs, kisses, and cheek pinching—a somewhat traditional Italian good-bye for babies. Being surrounded by so much love and attention was the perfect formula for raising a happy and well-adjusted baby. Once Anthony was put to sleep, the family was treated to a meal prepared by Louise and Nanny. It was a long day for Louise, but she and Sal loved showing off their baby and relished the idea of being surrounded by family. They knew that a close and warm family environment was crucial to the healthy development of a child; it was the right way—the Italian way!

Louise's maternity leave was soon over and it was time for her to return to her teaching position. She was confident that her child would be well cared for by her mother while she was out of the house, but felt reluctant to be separated from him at such a young age. She knew her job was needed to maintain the family, yet she sensed a feeling of separation anxiety. She so loved the closeness and bonding of the daily routine of childcare. As time went on, her mixed emotions vanished and she was able to adjust to her role as a working mother. At the end of the school day, she would return home and resume her motherly duties. She would attend to the baby's needs while her mother prepared dinner. At the end of the evening, after Anthony was in his crib, Louise and Nanny settled down to a relaxing interaction of conversation, while Sal engrossed himself in his studies. Louise's week was full of teaching during the day and mothering in the evening, while Nanny's days were filled with cooking and childcare. On the weekends, Louise would have her mother go visit her sisters and brothers in Brooklyn and spend the night. She would return on Sunday evening, well-rested, and lovingly resume her role as Nanny.

Life was simple; work and home were the routine, all was peaceful, and everyone was content. All that occupied their minds was building a future and fulfilling their dreams. They felt secure and confident that their struggles and sacrifices would ultimately lead them to the end of the rainbow—a life filled with family and prosperity. Once again, tragedy struck America with the outbreak of World War II. Suddenly they were thrust into insecurity and fear; aspirations and dreams were replaced with uncertainty and despair—life was at a standstill as the whole world was engulfed in turmoil. The growth and prosperity of America was halted and the whole country was encapsulated in a shroud of panic and trepidation—the land of plenty was converted to food rationing and victory gardens. Industry and manufacturing switched gears and turned into a giant war machine. Women replaced men in the factories and families were separated as men went off to battle. A nation disrupted and a world fragmented and on the brink of destruction and chaos.

Louise was afraid that Sal would be drafted and sent off to fight in Europe, a common fear shared by many young wives. Her fears were for Sal and the possibility of losing him and their child growing up without a father. She became despondent over the thought that such an upheaval in the world could shatter their dreams. She was familiar with hard times and sacrificing, and she knew she had the strength to endure; nonetheless, she felt apprehensive and forlorn. She knew the future was promised to no one, and her family was in jeopardy. Sal registered with the draft board; they held their breath, put their plans on hold, and waited for his call to duty. A few months later, Sal received a letter from the draft board exempting him from active service due to his status as a teacher, even though he was a part-time substitute. They both breathed a sigh of relief as their fears were laid to rest. Their lives would be able to continue, but their worries still existed for the outcome of the war and the devastation it would have on humanity.

Like so many families during the war, Louise and Sal did their part on the home front to support the war effort; they planted victory gardens, sold war bonds, and limited their meat consumption through rationing. Both, having lived through the Great Depression, were accustomed to sacrifice and sustaining themselves on limited provisions. Louise was an expert at preparing sumptuous meals out of paltry ingredients. Give an Italian a few tomatoes, some garlic, and olive oil, and you have a feast! She knew how to stretch food, and leftovers were commonplace: waste not, want not was the motto. Most American families did not suffer from conserving; it was just a matter of getting along on less, not wasting, and cutting back on certain extravagances.

Louise and Sal went about their lives in a somewhat normal way, trying to squeeze some enjoyment out of each day. Family gatherings were still a normal routine, certain holidays took on new meaning, and special prayers were said for family members who were away in the military. Anthony continued to receive love and attention from all the relatives; however, he now had to share that attention with new cousins as the family grew. Sal's brother, Ray, now had a son, also named Anthony, and Louise's sister, Peggy, had a son named Louis. Anthony loved having cousins as playmates during the family gatherings; he, being the eldest, was the leader of the troupe—the Indian chief and his wild band of renegades. Excitement and noise were their missions and they knew how to supply plenty of both. They were in perpetual motion, only stopping when exhausted and finally asleep, only to return wide-eyed and bushy-tailed the next morning and back on the warpath. Johanna, the only girl, was the Indian princess and the boys were the warriors—each living his role to the fullest. Somehow, their parents managed to enjoy themselves in spite of the noise and commotion.

Knowing that when Lou and Peggy came down from Vermont for the holidays that Lou would want to be with his brothers and sister, Louise would have the whole "clan" over to celebrate. She and her mother would prepare the special holiday meals for what seemed like a cast of thousands. The dining room table was spread into the living room, the adults engaged in conversations, and Anthony and his wild band encircled the assemblage. The table was a cornucopia of Italian food whose aroma permeated the air.

The family, as usual, was treated to the skills of Louise's culinary expertise: a variety and abundance of Italian delicacies for dinner and special homemade deserts prepared by Nanny. Lou's brother, Tony, would supply the fresh pastries from Brooklyn. And yes, they all toasted "Salute!" with a glass of *Strega!*

Louise loved being hostess to her family and the new expanding families. She did it with such ease and finesse and with genuine warmth and love—it was her special gift to *"la famiglia."* Holidays were always special when Louise was growing up and she felt that she wanted her family and all the new children to be part of a beautiful and loving tradition. Holidays are a special time, a time for bonding, and a time for sharing. Louise shared her love with everyone and made everyone feel special—she was the consummate homemaker, party pleaser, and family diplomat. She never exalted herself; she always put other people first. She would always try to prepare the favorite dish of a particular guest, something special that they rarely ate or remembered from their youth. She loved to see their eyes open wide and the smile on their faces when she presented the meal. Louise was able to cook both the Neapolitan and the Sicilian-style dishes, making everyone happy.

Family gatherings and holidays were the only source of entertainment for Louise and Sal. Their work and family responsibilities plus a limited income left little opportunity for any outside expenditures. Everything was centered on the home and raising a family. Louise would spend her evenings sewing while Sal studied; they were peaceful and tranquil evenings once Anthony was put to bed. On the weekends, Sal would take courses at New York University and Nanny would visit her brothers and sisters in Brooklyn. Louise would tend to Anthony's needs and catch up on the household chores. She always found time to pursue her passion of designing. Since Johanna was the only girl out of all the children, Louise would design and make all her little party dresses. Johanna looked like a Dresden doll with all the latest styles and colors. Louise also made dresses for her mother and aunts, always making sure they were stylish and up-to-date. Deep down inside, Louise had hoped that she would someday have a daughter for whom she could sew. She knew that having another child now, especially with the war still raging in Europe and their financial situation, would be impractical and ill-timed.

Once again, God surprised Louise—she was pregnant with her second child. She was ecstatic and hopefully anticipated that she would give birth to a baby girl. Both Louise and Sal were overjoyed and somehow not as frightened this time as they were before. They knew that things always had a way of turning out for the good. They knew their home was secure; they had the help of Nanny. Louise would be able to return to work after giving birth, and Sal's odd teaching jobs would help carry the family. Sal was still trying to get a permanent teaching position so he could contribute more to the family income and utilize his language skills for which he had studied so hard all those years. Louise kept encouraging him and supporting him; she knew that some day languages would be in style and popular in the city schools, especially since so many foreigners were immigrating to America.

Louise continued teaching throughout her pregnancy while Sal struggled through his studies and sporadic teaching and tutoring assignments. That winter, Sal was given a golden opportunity to use his language skills and at the same time be of service to his country. Since he was fluent in French, he was asked to teach at Governor's Island in New York. Not knowing why, but thankful for the opportunity, he reported for duty. His assignment was to teach military officers the French language on an accelerated basis, as well as the local customs and geography of France. The war in Europe was apparently winding down and the last campaign was to be the liberation of France. The allies were preparing for a massive invasion of France, hoping that it would bring an end to Germany's domination of Europe. Sal was not privy to the logistics of the invasion, but he knew it was imminent. He was very proud to have such an important and vital role in the war.

Sal spent countless hours and days at Governor's Island, teaching day and night. Louise did not know the details of his assignment—Sal was not permitted to reveal any vital information about his job. She knew it was important, but not to what extent. As the months dragged on and Louise was drawing closer to her delivery date, she became more and more tired and weak. Anthony, being the active child he was, would love to jump up on to his mother's stomach when she was sitting and resting. Louise, fearing that he might hurt the baby, told him that she had a baby growing in her stomach and that he had to be gentler, so as not hurt her or the baby. Anthony understood what she said and quickly informed the neighborhood children that his mother had a baby growing in her stomach—much to the dismay of the neighborhood parents and forever dispelling the myth of the stork delivering babies.

It was late in May that she stopped teaching and was forced to rest in preparation for her delivery date. Louise rested most of the day, and in the evening, she and her mother would listen to the radio. News of the war was constantly being broadcast, and listening to the progress of the war was an everyday event. On June 6, 1944, the allied forces stormed the beaches of Normandy, France, in the largest invasion in the history of warfare, the D–Day invasion. Louise was listening to the vivid details of the invasion and the gruesome details about the death and destruction that was occurring. Tears ran down her checks as she heard of the countless American soldiers that were being maimed and killed. She empathized with all the mothers whose sons were being lost and crippled in battle, and suddenly realizing that in all her preparation for childbirth, she had never selected a name for the baby if it were to be a boy; she had been hoping for a girl. Louise decided that if she were to give birth to a boy, she would give the baby a name beginning with the letter "D" to commemorate the D-Day invasion.

Since Sal had so many French books in the house, Louise picked up a French history book in hopes of trying to find the location of Normandy, France, and familiarize herself with the area. While reading the history of France, she came across the region of Normandy and noted that the patron saint of Normandy was named St. Dennis. She knew at that moment that if she were to give birth to a boy, she would name him Dennis to commemorate D-Day and the American soldiers who were dying on the beaches of Normandy. When Sal came home from his assignment that evening, Louise informed him that she had chosen the name Dennis if she were to give birth to a boy. Sal had wanted a more traditional Italian name, but understood Louise's emotion and patriotism. Sal added a French middle name, Roland—a name associated with strength and courage for one of the Knights of the Round Table. Five days later, on June 11, 1944, I was born and given the name Dennis Roland. Mom felt proud that her new baby's name was a tribute to the fallen soldiers of the war, and yet deep down in her heart she feared that someday her sons might be called to battle.

A few weeks later, I was baptized in the new church that was built, and Mom and Dad celebrated the christening with the usual regalia of the Italian tradition. Aunts, uncles, and cousins attended the festivities and celebration. All the cousins played around me, but Johanna, in particular, paid special attention to her new baby cousin—she loved to hold and cuddle me; to her I was like a new toy doll. The whole family partook in the celebration and toasted to my health with *Strega!*

Chapter 4

Louise: Both Mother and Father

The war ended shortly after my birth, bringing an end to the turmoil in Europe. A new era was on the horizon with hopes of more growth and prosperity for America. Mom and Dad were hopeful for the future of themselves and their children. Mom returned to teaching, Dad continued his studies and part-time jobs, and Nanny now had two grandchildren to help raise. Everything seemed to return to normal with soldiers returning home and re-entering the job force and wives resuming their positions as mothers and homemakers. There were plenty of jobs to be had for the returning veterans and industry continued to flourish. Dad, on the other hand, still felt the frustration and disappointment of not being able to use his language skills in a financially secure position. He felt at a dead end in his career and became despondent, especially seeing so many new jobs opening up for the veterans. Knowing he had another mouth to feed with the birth of his new son, he entertained thoughts of leaving teaching and entering the industrial job market. Both Mom and Dad were saddened over the prospect of him abandoning his studies and forgoing a career in teaching.

Right before Dad decided to leave teaching, Lou called from Vermont with the news that the city of Rutland was opening up a junior college and they were in need of a foreign language professor. Dad saw an opportunity to stay in teaching and use his language degrees in a prestigious position. Mom and Dad lamented over the opportunity, knowing that they would have to leave New York and that Mom would have to abandon her tenured teaching position. They were also saddened over the fact of leaving family and friends behind. They were in a quandary and all seemed hopeless. Mom knew how important Dad's career was to him and that his position as a professor would bring him respect and a sense of fulfillment. To Mom, there was only one solution, one that would split the family on a temporary basis. Since the position at the new college was a new project and there were no guarantees of the college becoming a permanent institution, they decided that they would keep their home in New York, and Mom would keep her teaching job. Dad would go to Vermont and live with Peggy and Lou. Mom knew it would be a sacrifice and an emotional hardship on the family, but it was the only way they could ensure their financial security while Dad tested the waters in a new poison and a new environment.

Mom knew how important it was for her to maintain a healthy and loving home environment for her children while Dad was away establishing himself in Vermont. She realized that she not only had to be the breadwinner of the household, but that she had to be both mother and father to her two sons. She was secure in the fact that her mother was able to help raise the boys while she was teaching and that they were loved and well cared for during her absence. When she came home from school, she took over and gave her concentrated attention to Anthony and me. She would help with the meals, play games with us, change diapers, and finish the night with comical Donald Duck bedtime stories. Her days and nights were long and full—but they were incomplete without her husband. Mom was used to sacrifice and hard work; it was part of her nature and she adapted well. She devoted her weekends to my brother and me, filling our day with activities and family gatherings. Every few months, Mom would take us on the train to see Dad in Vermont. We would leave late in the afternoon on Friday and return Sunday night. It was always a special get-together with Dad, and Mom was happy to be with her husband. Aunt Peggy was also happy to see her sister and nephews. Aunt Peggy was excited at the prospect of all of us moving to Vermont if Dad's position at the college materialized into a permanent and lasting position. She missed having family with her in Vermont and knew how wonderful it would be for her and mom to be together again as a family.

Holidays were spent in New York; Dad would drive down from Vermont with Uncle Lou, Aunt Peggy, Johanna, and Louis. It was always a houseful, all of Uncle Lou's family and Mom and Dad's family. The dining room table would extend into the living room—it was wall-to-wall table filled with the special meals prepared by Mom and Nanny. The house was saturated with love and warmth, and special lasting memories. Mom made sure that all the relatives were happy and content—the main thing for her was that we were all together as one big family. It was her special way of conveying love to her family and preserving the traditions she cherished. Everyone knew mom was the cohesive component of the family, and they loved and respected her for that.

Dad would return to Vermont after the holidays and once again, Mom would assume her dual role as mother and father until our next visit with him. Mom missed Dad, but she was fortunate to have family close by and good friendly neighbors to help fill the void. Living next door to us were Charlie and Frances, with their two daughters, Diana and Fonzi. Charlie and Frances were older than Mom was and Diana and Joan were teenagers. Frances would come over and visit with Nanny while Mom was at school. I would sit and listen to them speaking Italian and watch them while I played on the floor. Mom would come home from school and join in on the gathering. We all became very close—just like family. Diana was especially happy to have Mom as a neighbor because she was the recipient of a professionally designed, original prom grown. In the late afternoons, Mom would have Diana over and drape and design her gown. Diana was very petite, so Mom would have her stand on the dinning room table as she pinned and fitted her gown. What mattered to Mom was that it made Diana happy and it filled her evenings with her passion for designing.

Charlie became somewhat of a father figure to us; he was a warm and wonderful man. He looked out for us and helped Mom and Nanny by supplying them with the choicest meats from his butcher shop. We all shared many family dinners together. Dad loved speaking Sicilian with Charlie and Frances when he was home from Vermont. Mom and Dad felt very comfortable with them; their relationship reminded them of the old neighborhood where they grew up. Even though Mom felt secure in having such good neighbors, she still longed to have Dad back home. Dad knew his absence was hard on Mom and us, but he was determined to establish himself and become the breadwinner for his family. He realized it was sink or swim—this was his window of opportunity, his chance to achieve the fruits of his long struggle and arduous schooling. He missed his family and he missed New York, but he loved the beautiful mountains and crisp air in Vermont. He made the best of his situation, waiting for that pot of gold at the end of the rainbow.

Mom continued teaching and hoping that Dad would soon be settled so they could finally be together again as a family. She didn't want to leave New York and give up her job and leave her relatives and friends, but she knew her place was with her husband. She counted the hours, days, and weeks that rolled by, hoping for some word that Dad would soon be able to send for us. One day, while she was at school, her principal, who was familiar with Dad's language background, informed Mom that the New York City high schools were adding Spanish to their curriculum. Mom notified Dad that they were offering a full-time teaching license for languages in New York—something he had waited for all these years. He was now faced with a decision; stay in Vermont or go back to New York. He knew that his place was in New York with his family. Dad came home, took the exam for licensure, and was appointed to a school close to home. We were a family together once again.

Mom and Dad, now both fully licensed teachers, went about their lives and everything was normal. Weekends, once again, were filled with family gatherings of friends and relatives. Charlie helped us complete our little family by surprising us with a little puppy who we named Cherie. She was a mutt, all fluffy and white. She was the new family member and responded to Nanny in Italian and us in English—I guess you could say she was a bilingual dog. Dad had a fence built in the backyard for Cherie, and put a gate between our house and Charlie's so we could pass between houses easily. Many meals were cooked outside on the barbeque and shared between the families. Relatives from both families mingled together, making one big happy family. Charlie supplied the meat and Mom and Nanny made the pasta and side dishes, once again and always a feast. Anthony and I were fortunate to have grown up in such a warm and loving atmosphere. We were always surrounded by relatives and friends and learned the true meaning of family. Our parent's closest friends were called aunt and uncle, and our cousins were like brothers and sisters. We learned respect for our elders and that everyone in the family was important.

New neighbors, Hy and Sylvia, along with their two daughters, Diana and Margie, and Sylvia's mother, moved next door to us on the other side of our house. A new warm and loving relationship soon evolved. Diana was Anthony's age and Margie was a little younger than I was. Mom and Dad had them over for dinner often and exposed them to the Italian cuisine. They spent many holidays with our family, including the religious ones, and we shared many Jewish holidays in their home as well. Mom always taught us to respect each other's religious beliefs. Dad and Hy got along great—they were both kibitzers and one tried to outdo the other. Mom and Sylvia were like sisters, both sharing stories about their children and husbands. Anthony and I got along with the girls as best we could for pre-adolescents. We didn't really know how to play with girls at that age, so we treated them like boys. Over the years, the two families grew closer and Anthony and I became closer to the girls in a healthy brother/sister way. Sylvia's mother and Nanny also became very friendly and close to each other. They would sit on the front porch and wait for us to come home from school. They rocked in their chairs and exchanged intermittent words to each other; one speaking Italian and the other speaking Yiddish—somehow they understood each other. They smiled and made gestures; somehow, they found a comradeship.

Mom taught school throughout the year and spent her evenings preparing lessons, paying bills, and playing with my brother and me. Dad was back at New York University taking more courses in preparation for a principal's position. His principal recognized that he had a flair for administration and encouraged him to further his career. Dad took courses on weekends and studied at night, while Mom took care of the household affairs. On weekends, Mom would occupy us with sports—Anthony would play little league and I would watch. She even enrolled us in dance lessons to give us poise and refinement. Mom made sure we were occupied so Dad could study.

Since Mom and Dad loved the Vermont countryside so much, they decided to spend their summers there. They were off from school for two months, giving us the opportunity to leave New York during the sweltering and sizzling summer months and enjoy the crisp, cool mountain air. They bought a summer home on a lake in the remote town of Belmont, Vermont, with a population of 200 people. The unpainted wooden cottage was very primitive: no bathroom, no drinking water, no telephone, and no heat. We had to fill up gallon cans of drinking water at the general store down the road. The bathroom was an outhouse without electricity twenty-five yards from the house. There was one sink in the kitchen supplied with undrinkable water from the lake and powered by a small outside pump.

At the end of the school year, Mom and Dad would pack a trailer hooked up to our car with canned food, clothes, toys, and Dad's books and off we went on the eight-hour expedition to the mountains. We would all pile into the car: Mom, Dad, Nanny, Anthony, and I, and of course the dog. Mom would make pepper and egg sandwiches for lunch along the way. It was an adventurous and torturous ride along winding hilly roads. The exodus from New York ended with a car full of exhausted and carsick pioneers. Once the trailer was unpacked, we started the rough and rugged adventures of country living.

Even though Belmont was beautiful and Mom was glad to leave the sweltering summer heat of New York, it was not a real vacation for her. She worked around the clock just for the basic comforts of daily living. There was no hot water to wash dishes or do laundry. She had to boil water on the stove to wash dishes, and did the laundry in a tub, and rinsed them off in the sink. The clothes were hung outside to dry on a line between two trees. The refrigerator was an old-fashioned icebox, large enough only for milk, eggs, and butter. All the groceries had to be purchased fresh daily.

Drinking water was used sparingly from the tin gallon cans. Every morning, Mom would walk down the dirt road to the general store with my brother and me to fill up two gallons of water and buy the fresh produce for the day. We also stopped by the local post office to check our mailbox for mail. The return trip back up the road was interrupted by several stops along the way to rest from carrying all the packages and heavy cans of water. Once back home, Mom would make a breakfast cooked on a two-burner electric stove.

Dad would spend his mornings clearing the land of rocks, trees, and hay. His afternoons and evenings were occupied by his studies. Mom was not only chief cook and bottle washer; she was the entertainment director for my brother and me. She would take us swimming on the little town beach by the lake next to our cottage. She also took us on hikes up the mountain road and across cow pastures. Mom filled our days with activities and when we were done playing, she would clean, cook, and do laundry. At the end of the day, she was exhausted, but she always had time to tell us our bedtime stories. After we were put to sleep, she would sew and mend cloths while Dad studied. Summer nights were cold in the mountains; heat from a kerosene stove helped relieve the chill. Even though everyday living was somewhat primitive, Mom and Dad were content with their little cottage in the mountains.

Aunt Peggy would drive out to the cottage from Rutland with Johanna and Louis during the day. While she visited with Mom and Nanny, we all played and ran all over the place. Sometimes, we would go for a boat ride on the lake or horseback riding by the barn down the road. We often went on hikes up old dirt roads that led up the mountains, picking crabapples from the trees along the way. Mom would make us all lunch and the children would eat outside in a makeshift tent made from old bed sheets. We learned how to have a good time with the simple things in life. We learned a lot about country living; we learned to ride horses, row boats, hike, chop wood, cook outdoors on an open camp fire, milk cows, feed chickens, and rake hay. We became gentleman farmers at a young age. It was undoubtedly better than spending the summer months in the hot and steamy inner city.

On Sundays, Uncle Lou and Aunt Peggy would drive out for Sunday dinner. Mom did her best to make the traditional Italian dinners despite the limited cooking facilities. She cooked some of the food on the outdoor fireplace. After dinner, we all sat around the fireplace; the adults engaged in conversation while we rascals toasted marshmallows on the open fire. Mom enjoyed having the family out for Sunday dinner; it reminded her of back home in New York. Since I was the youngest of all the cousins, I was left out of many of the older boy activities. Anthony and Louis would take off and roam the countryside while I was left alone to play by myself. Sometimes, Louis stayed overnight, and he and Anthony would sleep outside in the clubhouse Dad had built for us; I was too young for that adventure. Aunt Peggy, being sensitive to my being left out, would have me return with them to Rutland and spend a few days at their house. It was like a return to civilization—indoor bathrooms and television. On the drive back to Rutland, Uncle Lou had to stop at the hospital to check on his patients. He had me tag along with him while he went from patient to patient. It was then that I learned how to empathize with and become sensitive to people's needs. Uncle Lou was gentle, kind, and caring toward his patients; his calm and consoling manner seemed to ease patients' pain. He always introduced me to the nurses and his patients as a future doctor. He gave me his first stethoscope—a talisman so to speak—in hope that I would someday pursue a career in medicine. He was an icon, a man certainly worthy of emulating.

The large family get-togethers and feasts of plenty did not subside just because Mom and Dad were away from New York. Every few weeks, a caravan of relatives and friends from New York would descend upon the quiet and tranquil countryside like a stampede of wild, hungry horses. Their cars were stuffed full of food from Italian grocery stores; delicacies that were impossible to get in Vermont. They all knew that Mom could turn the raw ingredients into a sumptuous feast fit for kings. Some of the people would stay at our house, and others would stay in nearby motels or boarding houses. During the day, they all camped out at our place, taking advantage of the lakeside activities or relaxing on the lawn in hammocks and chairs. Dinnertime was a spectacle to see; picnic tables were lined up from end to end across the lawn, stone fireplaces blazing with hot charcoals, and monster pots of boiling water. In one pot would be dozens of country fresh corn-on-the-cob and in another would be five pounds of spaghetti. The grill would be heavy with pounds of fresh Italian sausage and cut up chicken parts. Inside mom's tiny kitchen, she would be preparing the spaghetti sauce and other side dishes to add to the array of homemade food.

Once dinner was served, it was like a free-for-all of ravenous, shipwrecked voyagers finding food. The crisp mountain air had a way of opening up one's desire for food. As soon as one dish of food disappeared from the table, another would appear, making it a continuous flow of mouthwatering pleasure. There were plenty of beverages to quench the thirst of everyone. The homemade wine flowed freely and endlessly. "U*no pranzo sensa vino e como uno giorno sensa sole*"; a dinner without wine is like a day without sunshine. Ice-cold watermelons, fresh pastries from Brooklyn, and homemade country pies topped off the meal. The dinner would last for hours, culminating with everyone being happy, content, and soporific. Mom would clean up the dishes with the help of some of the women; the men would sit around talking, and the children would play and run around. Everyone huddled around the barn fire as the sun began to set and the chill of the evening air crept in. The men would start singing and harmonizing their old favorite songs—their melodious resonance echoed through the mountains in the quiet night air. The hills were alive with the sound of music!

The summer months were full of plenty of activities and weekend guests. Mom was always busy with keeping my brother and I occupied, and Dad was busy with his studies and gentleman farmer chores. We were always doing something outside, whether it was swimming, hiking, boating, or horseback riding. Being outside in the fresh mountain air made us all sleep like babies at night. Dealing with the lack of city comforts seemed to settle in and we all learned to adjust to our environment. Anthony and I learned a lot about country living and grew to love the open fields and mountain streams.

We both made summer friends our own age and found consolation in the fact that we were all living a healthy and clean life in the mountains.

At the end of the summer, we packed up the trailer and reluctantly made the tortuous drive back to the city. Mom was anxious to get back to the city where she had all the modern conveniences, but Anthony and I were not happy to return and start the new school year. We knew playtime was over and the reality of school saddened us. We held on to the dream of returning next summer and having the run of the land. Mom and Dad also looked forward to returning, but they made plans to modernize the cottage so it would be more comfortable and less primitive. They knew that someday they would retire, and that spending more than just the summer months in Vermont was a viable option. Mom and Dad planed to bring the cottage into the twentieth century.

Every subsequent summer brought new changes to the cottage in Belmont. The first major project was having an indoor bathroom. It's amazing how such a simple thing could make such a big difference in living. They also had a well dug so we could have hot and cold running water for cooking and drinking. Mom got a new stove with an oven and a real refrigerator. These items made Mom's life a little better and easier for her to entertain the constant flow of friend and relatives that made Vermont their habitual retreat. There was always some form of renovation or project going on throughout the summer. As Anthony and I grew older, we had to contribute the physical labor for a good part of the refurbishing. Mom was the supervisor; she planned our workday, and after so many hours of what seemed like slave labor, we were allowed to go and play with our friends. Since the winters were extremely harsh in Vermont, it was necessary to paint the exterior of the cottage every summer to protect the wood. We also had to help clear the land so we could eventually have a true lakefront house. Every year we inched our way down to the lake by chopping trees, moving rocks, and cutting brambles and bushes.

Over the years, the cottage was transformed into a showplace, with beautiful and copious flower gardens and lush green grass flowing down to the lake. The inside was totally renovated with larger rooms and giant picture windows overlooking the lake and mountain ranges. New walls and insulation added to the coziness as did the huge indoor wood burning fireplace.

All the conveniences of modern country living made it a mountain paradise. Everyone who came to visit felt as if they were in seventh heaven. Mom and dad enjoyed having people stay over, they were very proud of their new summer palace. Mom continued to have large family get-togethers and treated all her visitors to enormous and sumptuous meals, and always ending with a glass of *Strega*.

Belmont became a retreat, a refuge to sooth your mind and replenish your spirit. Mom and Dad seized every opportunity to sneak away to the mountains. Every school holiday was a pretext to get away and get pleasure from the beautiful seasons of Vermont. Fall was especially beautiful with the myriad of colors that painted the mountainside. The brilliant red and orange colors blending with the dark evergreen pines were a landscape from an artist's pallet. It was nature's magnificent beauty at its best. The crisp mountain air blending with the deep blue sky and painted autumn leaves left you mesmerized.

There was much more that added to the beauty of Vermont than the scenery and clean mountain air. It was the closeness with family that made it a truly wonderful experience. Mom relished being with Aunt Peggy and Uncle Lou, and Anthony and I developed a close and enduring bond with our cousins. The love and caring of family was paramount in our development and maturation. Mom made sure that we shared valued experiences and togetherness, deep and meaningful love, and a sustained loyalty to family—*la famiglia!*

Chapter 5

GROWTH, CHANGE, RELATIONSHIPS: DEEP AND ENDURING

To all of us, Vermont was a fantasyland and New York was a humdrum reality. Vermont offered my brother and me real change and a chance to mature and develop. We were unencumbered by congested city living and structured school restrictions. The driving age started at fourteen years old with an adult driver seated next to you. We were able to learn to drive on empty country roads and wide open highways. It was a giant step from bicycles to cars; a leap into the beginning of the adult world. Anthony was the first to experience that growth spurt and he plunged ahead with a full head of steam. Once he entered that magical world of teenage privileges, there was no holding him back. Mom and Dad had their hands full; from the little wild Indian as a child, to the precocious pioneering adolescent, he was a force to be reckoned with. He always had a propensity for enjoying life to its fullest. Tony, as he wanted to be called, was always happy, carefree, and capricious; never despondent or morose. He was a leader, never a follower, always taking charge and plunging ahead in the direction of the pursuit of happiness. I looked up to my older brother, hoping someday to be able to emulate him. Every child has an idol, a role model, a hero; Tony was all that to me.

Mom and Dad also experienced change, now having a growing family and more responsibilities. Adults grow and deal with more change as they and their families mature. Life itself is a never-ending maturation process, full of excitement, joy, frustration, and sadness. It's how one handles the process that makes a person glide through life either unscathed or scared.

During the regular school year, we all had our areas of responsibility; Dad still studied and taught, Tony and I struggled through classes, and Mom taught her fashion design classes at the local high school. She enjoyed her classes, but she felt that there was so much more her students could learn before going out into the fashion world. There were so many new technical and scientific aspects to fashion and design that were immerging during the industrial and manufacturing explosion in America. She knew that if her students were to be successful in the workforce, they would need to continue their education on a higher level, one that would make them more qualified and equipped to contribute to the growing industry. Since there were no four-year colleges offering degrees in fashion and design, Mom set out on a mission to explore the possibilities of creating an institution where talented students could attain a college degree and enter the fashion and design world with both technical and scholastic skills.

She, along with some of her teaching colleagues and designers from the industry, set out to obtain state approval and funding to start a college in Manhattan that would be committed to fashion, art, and design, as well as academics. It proved to be a long, complicated and arduous undertaking; filing state forms, seeking accreditation, obtaining charters, and licenses, and developing a curriculum that would meet state mandates. Their unselfish and tireless efforts came to fruition when they were finally granted a charter from the state education department. The college was founded and given the name, The Fashion Institute of Technology, better known as F.I.T. Mom felt very proud to have been one of the founders of what in latter years turned out to be a highly respected and well-known institution of higher learning. Every year mom would have her most talented high school students apply for admission, and indubitably, they would be accepted based not only upon their ability, but also upon mom's recommendation.

Dad advanced in his career after passing the principal's exam and completing numerous certification requirements and courses. He was appointed as an assistant principal in one of the nearby junior high schools in Queens. His long and committed efforts also catapulted him up the ladder in the world of academia. He was the first principal to introduce a bilingual program in Spanish into the city schools. His expertise in languages and extraordinary teaching skills made his program the model for the entire city school system. Dad's dedication and expertise won him accolades from every level of the city, from the mayor's office all the way to the state education department. Mom was very proud of Dad and she felt pride in knowing that her constant support and encouragement contributed to his success.

I clumsily stumbled through the early years of adolescence, dealing with the physical and social changes that plaque all young boys—voice change, lip hair, newfound muscles, and shyness around girls who smiled at me. All of a sudden, it was a new world, one filled with wonderful moments on the one hand and awkward and frightening moments on the other. No one escapes the ritualistic passage from boyhood to manhood without going through the gauntlet of development. School presented new challenges as I passed from grade to grade; more was expected of me from the teachers and boyish pranks were no longer tolerated. Growing up took on a new meaning, one filled with more responsibility and accountability.

Tony glided into the middle adolescent years with ease. He was at that magical age where he felt invincible and unbeatable in everything he did. He was an excellent athlete; he excelled in every sport he played, and gained the admiration and attention from all the neighborhood girls. His popularity, personality, and good looks were the perfect combination that made his social life an enviable experience. Tony was like the western cowboy stars on television who always ended up with the pretty girl; whether it was in New York or Vermont, he always had an entourage of beauties following him. At sixteen years old, he met and fell in love with a beautiful and popular cheerleader from Rutland, Vermont, named Judy. Tony knew when he first met Judy that this was not the puppy love that most teenagers go through. This was the real thing: a true and deeply-felt love that captured his heart and soul, and embroiled his mind.

The mid-1950s seemed to be a great time for growing up with the many new and exciting changes in America. The pre-war babies were now teenagers and discovering their own style of dress and a new kind of music that rocked the entertainment industry. It was an era of change that the adult world thought was ostentatious and superficial, and mixed with a wild unheard of use of the English language. It was the Flapper generation versus the Rock and Roll generation. Parents had a hard time dealing with their children and the children had a hard time convincing their parents that this was a normal transition for them. Mom had a different outlook on all these changes; having a musical background and remembering her own desires for modern music, she enjoyed the peppy new tunes. She also saw some hope for the new dress styles and welcomed most of the changes in a more conservative way. Nanny, on the other hand, was totally befuddled and bewildered, and thought the teenagers were the devil in disguise. She was able to deal with me a little better since I was still a pre-adolescent. The only difficulty she had with me was my name. She insisted on making my name sound Italian. She endearingly called me "De-na-sa" just because it sounded more Italian!

Mom always made sure that Tony and I were always dressed well and in style without being flamboyant or gaudy. She instilled in us a sense of fashion and an interest in always looking neat and presentable. Mom taught us at a very early age how to pick out clothing and how to match color and patterns. Whenever she took us shopping for suits, pants, or shirts, she always pointed out to us how the garment was made. We learned what to look for in a particular article of clothing; the way the sleeve was inserted at the shoulder, how the patterns lined up on the side of the garment, the evenness of cuffs and collars, and the way the lining was made. Mom made sure that we understood the meaning of "the well dressed man." We even had our own tuxedos to wear to weddings and special social events. Mom made sure that we made an elegant and meticulous transition from boyhood to manhood. She taught us grace, poise, and style; always making sure we made a good appearance.

Everything else in our family lifestyle remained pretty much the same. The family dinners and gatherings continued as usual, always an event to look forward to and a great time to be had by all. As the families grew, our interaction and evolvement increased. Friendships became more important and cherished, and deepened in meaning. Tony and I learned from mom and dad the importance of close friends and family by their example. Mom was always very loyal and committed to her friends, always concerned and interested in their happiness and welfare. It was a sensitivity that she possessed and handed down to all of us. It's all about caring for people, respecting them, and loving them. Her father had an expression in Italian, *"fa bene, dimenticare, fa malo, pensiero"*—do good and forget about it, do bad and worry about it. Always a clear and guilt-free mind!

Tony and I developed close relationships not only with our cousins but also with our friends. During the school year, we had close friends on the block where we lived in Queens and close friends during our summers in Vermont. Mom always made sure that we played fairly and were good to our friends—she taught us how to share and not be selfish. All of our friends liked Mom and she in turn was kind and motherly to them.

They liked playing at our house, especially when mom would make some sort of meal and have our friends stay for lunch or dinner. Since most of our friends were not Italian, they loved Mom's special array of Italian meals. It was always a treat for them to stay over and gorge themselves with the different kinds of spaghetti and all that went with it. To them it was a Roman feast; to us it was a normal dinner. Sometimes I wondered if our friends came over to play with us or to eat Mom's food. When we played in our back yard or in the driveway, they could smell the aroma of the food spewing from the open windows or exhaust vent. They gravitated to where the smell was coming from and would start salivating like Pavlovian dogs, hoping for an invitation to partake in the meal.

Tony was granted many more privileges than I was because he was older. He ventured off the block and had a wider neighborhood to roam, more friends and interesting places to explore. I was confined to up and down the block and I had to be in when the streetlights came on, not giving me much opportunity to discover new adventures or friends. Most of my friends lived a few houses away, making it a short trip by bike, and within earshot of mom calling me home. Margie next door used to come over after school and do homework or watch television with me while waiting for her parents to come home. Many of my friends made fun of me because I played with a girl, but she was a close friend and I ignored them. Mom insisted that I treat her with respect and act like a gentleman at all times. I tried to roughhouse it with her, but she was a real girl, not a tomboy, so I had to watch out for her and make sure she didn't get hurt. The most fun I had with Margie was during the Christmas holidays. She loved to come over and help me decorate the Christmas tree. It was our special tree; we each tried to outdo the other when adding the ornaments. When we were finished we gave each other a glance and a nod of satisfaction, and we both silently acknowledged our joint accomplishment. I was glad Margie could enjoy our holiday and feel the spirit of Christmas. Mom made sure that it became a tradition; the Christmas tree was always decorated with love by Margie and me.

Mom took on more and more responsibilities with her aunts and uncles as they advanced in age. Nanny was also getting up there in age and needed more assistance doing things. On Saturday mornings, Mom would accompany Nanny to Brooklyn so she could help her aunts and uncles with their household and personal matters. I would accompany Mom and Nanny on the long trek by bus and subway from Queens to Brooklyn. Once we were in Brooklyn, we had a five-block walk to where they lived. The neighborhood seemed out of the ordinary and strange to me, not like what I was used to in Queens; all the houses were attached and had no front yards. The house was right off the street with high stone porches and double entry doors. To gain entry you had to press a doorbell and be buzzed in. Once inside, the hallway was dark and narrow with a long and steep ascending staircase to the second floor. We were always greeted at the top of the stairs by mom's aunt Nicoletta, a petite and lovable matronly old woman. She would lead us to the front parlor where we would sit and begin our visit. They spoke in Italian and I would sit idly and listen to their conversation. Mom would take care of whatever had to be done, whether it was paying bills or making phone calls to set up appointments.

After we had lunch, Mom and I would leave for our journey back to Queens; Nanny would stay overnight and return Sunday evening. It was a long and tiring day for Mom and me. Once home, I would settle in and play outside while Mom made dinner for us. Mom was exhausted by the end of the day and would go to bed early; knowing the next day was going to be busy with family guests and Sunday dinner.

Mom really worked hard both day and night during the week and on weekends. It seemed like she never rested. She took on another challenge to add to her exhausting schedule of teacher and homemaker. Since she had never received a full four-year college degree like most of the teachers she worked with, she decided to go to NYU at night to earn her B.S. in education. At the end of her teaching day, she would travel into Manhattan by bus and subway and attend two evening classes until 8:00 p.m. When she arrived home latter in the evening, Nanny would heat up whatever was leftover from the dinner she had prepared for the rest of us. It was an exhausting and strenuous program, but like every thing she undertook, she persisted and never wavered, and at the age of fifty, received her well-earned degree. She now had all the credentials necessary for advancement in the city school system. Later that spring, Mom was appointed head of the fashion design department at her school.

That same spring, Tony took a giant step into adulthood with the acquisition of a used car. He was the first in the neighborhood to achieve such a responsible and accountable honor. He became the king of the block with his 1948 black Mercury. He wasn't allowed to drive it within the city limits since he only had a junior driver's license, but at times, he and his friends somehow ventured out and cruised the streets without Mom and Dad finding out. All the guys on the block helped Tony get the car souped up with spinner hubcaps, bullnoseing the front hood, adding chrome dual exhaust pipes, and hanging dice from the rear view mirror.

That summer proved to be a fun-filled and carefree time for Tony. He and his friend Larry, along with a carload of other boys and girls, drove all over Belmont seeking out new and daring adventures up and down the winding and narrow roads of Vermont. Belmont was never the same; Tony and his friends woke up the tiny sleepy hollow village with the sounds of dual exhausts and rock and roll music blasting as they flew by the roadside cottages. The wild and thrill-seeking teenagers now gave their parents more reasons to be worried.

Tony extended his adventures outside Belmont, especially with dating his new girlfriend Judy. He was rarely around any more; he was always out, only returning for dinner, and back out again and off to Rutland to date Judy. Having a car at sixteen proved to be the catapulting event to Tony's romantic spree. No matter where he drove, Judy was always by his side, sitting in the middle of the front seat next to him. They were quite an item, and everyone knew they were boyfriend and girlfriend. I thought it was cool that my brother had a girlfriend, but I couldn't understand why he wanted to spend so much time with her instead of staying home and hanging around the town playing with his other friends. I guess at twelve years old, you look at things in a different way!

Mom had given Tony a curfew of midnight. She and Dad were worried about Tony driving at night along the eighteen mile unlit winding and curvy mountain road between Rutland and Belmont. Dad went to bed early every night after being exhausted from toiling in his large vegetable garden and keeping up with all the other yard work. Mom would wait up for Tony even though she too was exhausted from her long day of activities. She waited with bated breath until she would see the headlights of Tony's car glimmering in the distance on the approach to our cottage. Tony, more often than not, exceeded the deadline of his curfew, making his late-night escapades even more stressful and anguishing for Mom as she held her vigil peering out the window. I stayed up at night with Mom on many nights; I could see the worry and fear on her face and could almost hear the silent prayers she was thinking for her son's safe return. Mothers have an inherent ability to be fretful and an unambiguous knack in conveying their trepidation to their children. Tony, despite Mom's consternation and apprehension, shrugged off her firmness as being overly protective. That summer was a growing experience for all of us; whether we liked it or not, accepting change was part of the process.

The rest of the summer proceeded as usual with the inflow of friends and relatives from New York and the large family outdoor gatherings. The only difference was the pleasant and delightful presence of Judy; she was now a regular part of our lives and a very special part of Tony's. It was very hard for the both of them to say good-bye to each other at the end of the summer, but they knew they had shared something very special and meaningful and it was not going to fade away. Their feelings for each other would not vanish at summer's closing stages. The fires would still kindle long into the autumn and winter by lengthy letters and sporadic long-distance phone calls.

Chapter 6

Loss, Sadness, Heartache: Unwavering Strength

Time marches on and leads us all to new and uncharted waters. Sometimes our expectations of what the future holds for us are based on what we believe to be expected of us and at other times on what we fantasize it to be. We all hope that when we pass through life that it is a smooth and pleasurable transition and that we are spared any adversity along the way. Life seems so uncomplicated when you look through the eyes of a child, but as the years march on, the vision of simplicity becomes clouded with reality.

Mom and Dad had a vision for both themselves and my brother and me. They, like most families, always planned for their children's future and hoped for the best. Children often chart a course different from what is expected of them; not having the benefit of experience, they often take chances and try to circumvent reality. Mom was no stranger to reality and the hardships and anguish that it presents, knowing all too well that there are many thorns on the rose bush. She has dealt with distress and unhappiness all her life, always having the resolve to overcome any hardship that presented itself.

I was finishing my last year in grammar school and looking forward to starting high school in the fall. Tony on the other hand decided not to continue his education and go on to college, instead he wanted to take a break from school and serve in the military. Mom and Dad were very disappointed and saddened by his decision, but like many boys in the late 1950s, it was not uncommon to join the service and serve their country. Mom had always instilled in us a sense of patriotism and duty to our country. She was a great patriot and proud of her country and the freedom that America gave her and her family. She had always known and feared that someday her sons might be called to serve their country in a time of need, something she dread, but knew was necessary. Her only consolation at this time was that the United States was not at war and her son would not be in jeopardy. Despite the peacetime environment, she dreaded having her son leave home.

The day after mother's day, 1958, Tony left for the Army. It was a sad and solemn day for all of us; there was emptiness and a void in the house, a sense of an eerie stillness that filled the air. The house that was once filled with excitement and happiness now seemed quiet and cold. Tony was the center of attention for so long, now he was gone!

The day Tony left home for the army left me scared and lonely; my big brother and hero was no longer around to take care of and protect me. In a way, I felt proud of him becoming a soldier; having been brought up watching John Wayne war movies, I always admired soldiers. Tony and I shared a room growing up; we each had a single bed with a nightstand in the middle separating them. We shared a desk; the left side was mine and the right side was his. Now suddenly I had the whole room to myself; it was an uncomfortable and unusual feeling. The room seemed empty and I was frightened to sleep there all alone. I missed Tony and all the excitement he created.

Mom really felt his absence from the home, but it wasn't until the day she received a package in the mail from Fort Dix with all his civilian clothes in it that she broke down and sobbed. All I could do was hug her and try to sooth her sorrow. I guess it was seeing his clothes that triggered the realization that he was gone and not coming home for a long time. As she looked into my eyes and held me very tight, her cheek next to mine, I could feel the warm tears she was shedding cascading down my face. I cried with her and I felt the pain she was going through. Now I knew for the first time what real sadness felt like, that empty aching feeling in my heart frightened me and left me weak and scared.

The first two weeks during basic training in the army was a period of adjustment for the soldiers; they were not allowed visitors during that period. Once we were informed we could visit Tony, Mom went all out preparing all his favorite meals for the Sunday visit; she made enough food to literally feed an army. Mom stuffed all the food into airtight containers and we took off for Fort Dix. We had prearranged to meet Tony at a designated picnic area at the fort. When we arrived, there were thousands of soldiers all dressed alike; it seemed like a sea of soldiers descending on the picnic grounds. We looked and searched for Tony, hoping to spot him in the enormous crowd. All of a sudden, Tony appeared, walking toward us, tall as a giant and looking so handsome dressed in his army uniform. We all rushed up to him and hugged and kissed him—once again the Italian emotions spewed forth. Mom shed tears of joy seeing her soldier son; we all felt a sense of joy and pride in seeing Tony the soldier.

Every Sunday became a ritual for the next eight weeks; we would pack up all the food and descend on the fort like a food delivery service. All of Tony's soldier friends became accustomed to Mom's elaborate feasts and joined in with the rest of the family. Once again, Mom became the culinary entertainer, making special homemade meals that not only pleased Tony, but also delighted dozens of his homesick friends. Mom became the army mother to many lonely and hungry boys who were so far away from home. She enjoyed feeding the boys and she especially loved making her son happy.

Mom as usual became well-liked for not only for her cooking skills, but also because she showed each and every soldier that she cared for them. She knew they were lonely and missed home; it was her way of making them feel less homesick. I enjoyed being with my brother and all the soldiers and hearing of their week of rigorous training; it was always a beautiful day made perfect by Mom's special touch.

That fall I entered an all boys private parochial high school in Queens. It was quite a change from the grammar school I attended that was run by nuns. Brothers who were tough and strict ran Archbishop Molly High school. At first, I was frightened about going to high school, not knowing what to expect, but as time progressed, I became accustomed to the new challenges and the rigorous course subjects. I felt grown up but lonely in a sense, because I wasn't able to share and discuss my new role as a high school student with my brother. He was stationed on the west coast and we saw very little of him. Fortunately, I had a group of close friends who were going to the same school as me. We had been friends since kindergarten and we all lived in the same neighborhood. Every day Wally, Richie, Al, Tommy, and I would ride the same bus to school, and on weekends, we hung out together. We all shared the same experiences growing up and going through the maturation process. There was a strong bond between us and a loyal comradeship that was continuous and permanent.

Despite having close friends, I did miss my brother as an older role model in my life, I was hungry for a big brother image; someone to confide in and learn about what adolescents had to offer. In school, I gravitated toward two teachers who seemed to me to be ideal role models, each very different, yet both displaying strong moral fiber. Brother Leo was a giant of a man and former college football player from Massachusetts and Brother Ludwig was a good-looking, tough street kid from the Bronx. I looked up to and admired them both, and learned tremendous values from them. Brother Leo was very gentle and kind; very engrossed in helping you deal with adolescent problems in a soft and mild manner. Brother Ludwig gave you tough love; his approach was equally as effective but you had to go through the school of hard knocks to realize certain things.

Mom was happy that I had my close friends and the teacher role models in school. She sensed my feelings of missing my brother and knew that, while they could not replace my brother, they were the next best thing. She knew all my close friends all of their lives and she loved each and every one of them. She met my teachers and was very fond of them and appreciative for their surrogate brother role in my development.

That winter proved to be a very difficult and trying time for Mom, a period of extreme stress and sadness that would test her resolve and tenacity. Having always been the pillar of strength in the family gave her the capability to endure a multitude of hardships. Always stoic and yet gentile in her manner, she would tackle each situation with determination and steadfastness.

In early winter, Dad had a minor surgical procedure performed that resulted in an adverse outcome due to the post surgical effects of the anesthesia. He went into a deep depression and was left weak and listless, unable to return to school as a principal. He was incapable of doing anything and had to receive a tremendous amount of physical therapy and counseling. Mom, once again, had to be both mother and father to me during a crucial time of my development. I only had Mom to help and guide me during that period. Mom became exhausted teaching during the day, taking care of Dad, and dealing with me. To make matters worse, Tony informed us that he was being sent overseas to Germany for two years, further widening the gap between visits—once again splitting the family by a long distance separation. Mom, having the memory of World War II, was frightened for his safety, even though the war was long over. Tony was to be part of the occupation forces in Germany and she was concerned that hostilities could erupt once again in Europe. With Dad being ill, Tony's long-term absence exacerbated her feelings of loneliness and despair. Her energy now had to be focused on Dad and his recovery. We all missed Tony and hoped that things would soon get better and our happy family days would be restored. Over the next few months, Dad's condition improved slightly but not enough for him to return to work.

Nanny was getting up there in age; she was in her late eighties and her health was starting to fail. She was unable to move about as much any more, limiting her to more or less a sedentary role in the house. Now Mom had to cook and maintain the household for two incapacitated people and work full-time. I knew she was overburdened, so I tried to ease her burden by limiting my neediness and attention-seeking behavior. I saw the exhaustion and weariness in Mom's face, but I also saw the devotion and love that exuded from her as she went about her care giving duties.

Aunt Peggy had come down from Vermont to visit Dad and spend some time with Nanny. She knew Nanny was failing and she wanted to spend some time with her. Johanna was attending college in New Jersey at the time and she would often come to our house on the weekend and spend time with us. I looked forward to Johanna coming over; we shared many wonderful and happy times together. Mom always made Johanna feel like a princess and she would go out of her way to prepare her favorite homemade specialties. Since Aunt Peggy was down for a visit, Johanna seized the opportunity to come over on the weekend and see her mother. Even though Mom was worn out from her onerous duties, she made this visit special for everyone. It was a special feast with all the trimmings; it was partly a sad gathering, but nonetheless it was a family gathering. There was plenty of food as usual and of course, we toasted to everyone's good health and safety with *Strega!*

Even though it was a short visit, clouded with Dad's illness and Nanny's failing health, we all managed to get through the weekend. Johanna went back to school Sunday evening and Aunt Peggy left by car with a family friend the following morning. Everything went back to normal for the beginning of the day, a little sad because of everyone leaving, but for the most part, routine. Everything changed that evening when we received a phone call from Uncle Lou in Vermont. Aunt Peggy was involved in a terrible automobile accident on her way home in Benington, Vermont. She was critically injured; she had multiple fractures and a crushed hip. We were devastated by the tragic news. Mom did not tell Nanny for fear that it would shock her frail and elderly body, nor did she tell Dad, fearing it might worsen his mental state. Mom wept and sighed upon hearing of her sister's condition; another heartache and worry! I tried to console Mom as best I could, but I too was crying and upset—my favorite aunt who was always so kind and loving toward me was now suffering and in pain.

It was late spring. Dad's condition was improving, and he was back to work. Aunt Peggy was still in the hospital in traction and showing modest signs of improvement, and Nanny's health was deteriorating rapidly. Mom was still coping with all the heartaches, trying to keep everything in perspective while attending to all our needs. Her concerns were centered on Nanny and Aunt Peggy, now that Dad was better and working. I was finishing my first year of high school, preparing for my final examinations. Tony was serving his tour in Germany unaware of all the misery and turmoil at home.

While Tony was in Germany, our neighbor, Hy, went to visit him while traveling on business. Hy wined and dined Tony while in Europe, treating him like a son; he was always a loving and generous man. Hy called home while traveling abroad and was informed by his wife that Nanny's health was worsening rapidly. Before leaving Europe, Hy stopped off in Rome, Italy, on the last leg of his business trip. He made it a point to go to St. Peter's Basilica and purchased a pair of rosary beads for Nanny. He entered the Basilica while mass was being said and walked up to the altar holding the rosary beads in his hand. The priest came to the foot of the altar, suspecting Hy was not a Christian, and asked what his intentions were. Hy explained that he wanted the beads blessed for Nanny, who was very ill, hoping that the beads and the blessing from Rome would help her. The priest blessed the beads and Hy went on his way. When he arrived home in New York, he immediately came to our house and presented Nanny with the blessed rosary beads. He kissed her on the cheek and said he loved her and Nanny responded with a weak and feeble smile.

Mom, worried about Aunt Peggy and her condition, had been in close contact with Uncle Lou on a daily basis. She was not improving as well as they had expected and their fears were that she might never walk again. This was very disconcerting to all of us. Mom would also report to Uncle Lou how Nanny was progressing. In an effort to monitor Nanny's health, Uncle Lou asked me to describe her medical symptoms to him over the phone. He had me monitor her pulse and respiration every hour, and asked me to listen to her heart and lungs with the stethoscope that he had given me as a child. I described to him the types of sounds I heard and the rhythm of the heart beats. A few days later, based upon what I reported to Uncle Lou, we called an ambulance to take Nanny to the hospital. Later that night, during the early morning hours, we received a call from the hospital stating that Nanny had passed away. Mom and I went to the hospital to identify the body and see her for the last time. Mom was holding back the tears that were swelling in her eyes, trying to remain composed and prepared for the next few sorrowing days that lay ahead.

Mom and Uncle Lou decided that informing aunt Peggy of Nanny's death would only hinder her slow and torturous recovery. Mom made all the funeral arrangements for Nanny in Brooklyn, as she had done so many times before for all the relatives. Nanny was laid out in a beautiful casket with the rosary beads that Hy had given her. It was the first wake I had ever attended; I was filled with grief and sorrow to see my Nanny, knowing this was the final good-bye. The funeral mass was held in our local parish. I, along with my friend Wally, were the altar boys—a final and loving tribute.

Mom wrote a letter to Tony informing him of Nanny's passing a few days after the funeral. She didn't want to tell him earlier for fear he would try to make the long and difficult trip overseas. He wrote back expressing his sorrow; you could tell by his words that he was despondent and homesick. He was sorry he was unable to see her one last time and say good-bye. To all of us she is now a beautiful memory.

Mom and I went to visit Aunt Peggy in Bennington by bus; it was Mom's intent to tell her sister of Nanny's death in person. Upon arriving in Bennington, we checked into a local bed and breakfast, and immediately went to the hospital. We were greeted there by Uncle Lou, informing us that he had sedated Aunt Peggy to ease her suffering once Mom broke the news to her. Seeing Aunt Peggy in her private room, all bandaged up and in traction, was a shock to both Mom and me. She looked so frail and bruised, barely able to speak, yet she had a faint whisper of a smile on her face. I don't know how Mom managed to muster up the strength and composure to break the news to Aunt Peggy, but somehow in her stoic manner she told her. Aunt Peggy cried and expressed her regrets for not being there to see her mother one last time. It was a sad and solemn visit, but a necessary one. We spent most of the day with her, trying to console and lift her spirits. Mom's heart was breaking, looking at her sister in the condition she was in, wondering if she would ever be able to walk again. Mom gave her words of encouragement and ensured her that in time she would be back to her old self again. We left for home the next morning, very somber and emotionally weakened.

With the school year ending and our trip to Vermont for the summer on the horizon, Mom anticipated that it would be very different this year without Tony and Nanny's presence. All of us would feel the obvious void and emptiness; the lack of the hustling and bustling noise of a full house would unquestionably hush the once reverberating walls of the tiny cottage. Even though Mom needed that summer to be a period of healing and less chaotic, she realized that I might have a hard time being alone in Belmont. She knew how close I was with my friends and felt that it would be a good idea for me to have some companionship that summer to help alleviate my loneliness in light of the latest incidents. Mom invited my good friend Wally to come to Belmont and spend a few weeks with us, hoping that his presence would help perk me up and lessen my isolation.

Upon arriving in Vermont, Mom became aware that Aunt Peggy's recovery and rehabilitation was less than acceptable. She was in a state of depression and not responding to her physical therapy. The crushing impact to her hip and the lack of proper healing left her with a two-inch shortage of her right leg. Uncle Lou felt impotent and helpless in seeing his wife's inability to make an effort and struggle through the painfully grueling course of rehabilitation. Mom, always being the strong and indomitable one in the family, decided to take on the chore of Aunt Peggy's recovery. Mom converted the downstairs kitchen sitting area in the cottage into a bedroom and had her move in with us. She was determined to nurse her younger sister back to health and make her walk on her own. Mom was not going to allow her to remain depressed and crippled.

It was an uphill battle for Mom to get Aunt Peggy motivated to go through the arduous daily routine of painful stretching and leg exercises. Mom would lift her and have her hold onto a walker, trying to encourage her to take tiny steps on her own. Her progress was slow and tedious, but Mom was unrelenting and insistent that she undergo the rigorous and repetitive program. Day and night, hour after hour, Mom aided Aunt Peggy around the circular kitchen table, making an endless path, one exhausting step at a time, one after another. Mom did not heed her sister's pleas to quit, nor would she allow her to give up and lay inactive. Mom would dress her every day, comb her hair, and apply makeup in order to boost her morale and self-image. I watched as Mom tended to her sister's needs with such confidence and uncompromising love and care. Once again, Mom proved her tenacity and unwavering strength and love for her family.

My friend, Wally, had come up from New York to spend a few weeks with me. We made ourselves inconspicuous and unobtrusive as we occupied ourselves with horseback riding, boating, and middle-adolescent escapades. Mom tried to make Wally's visit as pleasant and enjoyable as she could, even though she was preoccupied with Aunt Peggy's care. We were left pretty much on our own, but yet we were under Mom's watchful eye; our adventures never exceeded her demand for cautiousness and prudence. Wally and I tried to experiment with our over-zealous and enthusiastic attempt of proving our manhood, but we never went beyond the boundaries of good sense. It was a very memorable and cherished time we spent together.

After several weeks of long and intense physical therapy and constant encouragement, Aunt Peggy started to show tremendous strides toward self-reliance and confidence in her ability to walk. Her demeanor and outlook became more positive and energetic; she now had the will and determination to overcome her handicap. Mom was very proud of her sister and her triumph over what seemed to be insurmountable obstacles at the time. Mom had Uncle Lou come over for dinner one Sunday that summer, telling him she had a surprise for him. When Uncle Lou arrived at the cottage he was greeted by Aunt Peggy, walking over to him with a slight limp, all dressed up, and smiling and composed, she hugged and kissed him. Uncle Lou's eyes swelled with tears as he glanced toward my mother, knowing that his wife was now intact again and back in his arms. We all celebrated that evening with a dinner prepared by Mom and Aunt Peggy; and of course, we finished off the meal with a glass of *Strega!*

Chapter 7

Expectations, New Roles, New Obligations

That fall seemed pretty much routine with all of us returning back to New York and back to the regular schedule of school. Nothing new for Mom and Dad, but new and exciting for my friends and me; we were starting our sophomore year of high school. Yes, we were the "know it alls," sophomoric in every respect, so we thought. Being fifteen years old and having one year of high school under our belt led us to believe we were privileged and beyond reproach. Well, we soon found out that the only things that changed were that more was expected of us in school, and we were no longer mollycoddled by our teachers and catered to by our parents. I, for one, tried to push the envelope with my parents, but Mom soon clipped my wings and screwed my head back on the correct way. She was the disciplinarian in the family, the one who set the rules, and she made sure you followed them.

Ever since she was a child, Mom took on responsibilities that enhanced her maturity and self-development. She was no stranger to hard work and learned the importance of appreciating how hard it was to earn money. Mom made sure I gained that respect for earning money. She insisted, instead of an allowance that was so freely given out to adolescents, that I earn my own money by taking on odd jobs in the neighborhood and at home. I took on many little jobs and was able to pay for most of my social activities such as bowling, movies, and school dances. I guess that was one of the privileges of growing up.

Responsibility comes in many ways; sometimes it is thrust upon you, and at other times, it is learned. That fall we had an opportunity to get away to Vermont during the Columbus Day weekend to witness the breathtaking and spectacular cornucopia of autumn colors that the countryside provided. My friend, Wally, joined us for what was to be a fun-filled getaway. Since I was allowed to drive a car in Vermont with an adult passenger in the front, Dad allowed me to take the wheel once we crossed the New York/Vermont border. I felt very grown-up, and of course, I had to show Wally how adept I was at driving. The narrow and winding mountain roads required constant alertness on the part of a driver at all times. The fall was especially hazardous due to an abundance of moist leaves that patterned the road surface. I lost control of the car on a sharp curve and careened into a roadside telephone poll. We were all in shock and panic; it was as if time stood still for several seconds. Once we regained our composure and realized what happened, we noticed our injuries. Dad had hit his face on the windshield, Wally had banged his forehead on the rearview mirror, and Mom had been thrust forward in the back seat, badly bruising her leg; I, oddly enough, escaped without any injuries. The car was a total wreck and the injuries were minor; or so we thought. Mom developed a severe blood clot in one of the veins of her leg, necessitating hospitalization. The doctors feared that if the clot dislodged, it could go to her brain or lung and cause a stroke or death.

Fortunately, after a few days in the hospital, Mom's clot dissolved and she was released. We stayed in Vermont for the rest of the week at Aunt Peggy and Uncle Lou's house. I was very devastated over the havoc and chaos that I caused, and bewildered over the fact that I had no recollection of the few seconds surrounding the collision. Mom and Dad were very understanding and forgiving, but I nonetheless felt tremendous guilt and remorse. Mom, in her stoic and poignant way, reassured me that sometimes things happen for a reason and that we should learn and benefit from our experiences. Our return trip to New York was uneventful and we all returned to our normal routines. For me, the learning curve took a giant step forward. Maturing and having more responsibilities not only meant more fun, it signaled a red flag; dangers are undeniably associated with our actions and we are accountable for those actions.

That Christmas was to be a special one for Mom; Tony was coming home for a thirty-day leave from Germany. Mom made sure that she planned every meal with exceptional care and attention and that she selected all of Tony's favorite dishes. So much sadness had happened in the family since he left home, this visit was to be the magic potion that would cheer everyone up. The preparations and holiday decorations started weeks in advance and consumed everyone's energy. All the relatives and friends also awaited Tony's arrival with excitement because knew that they would be treated to Mom's celebratory feasts in honor of her son. Mom always said, "If you want to make family happy, celebrate something and serve good food!"

Tony's arrival and vacation was all it was anticipated to be; every day was filled with merriment and festivities. I was able to relate to my brother in a different way; somehow being a teenager and in high school made him treat me more like one of the crowd, not the little brother he left two years ago. Mom seemed to treat him like an adult, noticing the maturity and wisdom he gained from being away form home. He was more somber and less juvenile, more secure and focused, and very self-assured and confident. The army has a way of making men out of boys, yet these characteristics are inborn and inherent; all you have to do is analyze Mom and realize the apple does not fall far from the tree! Mom was always a wonderful role model for self-determination and confidence; she was very decisive and never wavered from responsibly. She never let her sensitivity or emotions interfere with good judgment.

Tony's leave was over and he had to return to Germany for another fifteen months. We were all sad to see him leave but we knew that soon he would return home for good. He was in constant contact with us by numerous letters per week. He would fill us in on all his escapades around Europe with the friends he made while overseas. He developed a very close relationship with two boys: Marco, a cultured and sensitive boy from Youngstown, Ohio, and Mike, a rough and tough boy from Brooklyn. His detailed letters made us feel as if we were there with him and his friends. Mom was happy that Tony had established a good, close relationship with Marco and Mike; it made it easier being so far away from home and helped fill the void of being alone. I was always fascinated by the stories Tony wrote about Marco and Mike. I felt like I had two more older brothers, and oddly enough, I lived vicariously through their adventures.

Our lives at home continued with the normal routine of work and school. Johanna would come to spend weekends with us from college on a routine basis. It was wonderful having her stay with us; her visits were always exciting and pleasurable. Mom and Johanna had a special bond, more than a niece and aunt; Mom became her confidant and counselor. Living so far away from home, she cherished being pampered by Mom and listening to her motherly advice. Mom knew that a girl nineteen years old and away from home needed special consideration and guidance. Mom always seemed to have the solution to everyone's problems and knew how to lecture them in a loving and constructive way. To me, Johanna was more than a cousin, she was like an older sister; I always looked forward to the weekends when she would come to visit. We always had a lot of fun experiencing new and challenging adventures together. Mom would prepare a special meal on Sunday before Johanna would go back to school; we all toasted to everyone's health with a glass of *Strega!*

The rest of the school year flew by rapidly and our much-anticipated summer vacation loomed on the horizon. That summer was to be very different for me, not the usual hanging around and just having fun and frolicking on the beach. Mom, using her psychological and practical skills, insisted that I take the test for my Vermont driver's license. She felt that getting my license would diminish my fear to drive again since my accident, and that it would increase my self-confidence. She also insisted that I get a summer job to fill my time and make me more self-reliant. I passed my driver's test and got a job at the Rutland hospital as an orderly. I felt very independent driving to work every day, and I loved working with the doctors and nurses. Now sixteen, I felt like a grown-up, experiencing responsibility and hard work. I was exposed to many new challenges working with patients in the hospital; I developed a more compassionate and caring attitude toward people who were suffering from illnesses and pain and learned how devastating and heartbreaking it was to their families. It was very rewarding to be able to help people in need, something I always knew by observing my mother and how she cared for people.

Once again, with the summer ending, our migration back to New York took on the same expectations of a new but routine school year. I was to start my junior year of high school; Dad was appointed to a new school as principal; and Mom was given a new assignment as senior advisor to the students in addition to her regular teaching duties. Her new role would occupy much of her after school hours and personal time. Mom didn't mind her new assignment, she enjoyed the personal interaction with the students on a one-to-one basis and felt her life's experiences and advice would be very helpful in their development as young adults. Most of the students she helped came to her with academic problems and concerns with college admissions; however, there were quite a few girls that came to her with emotional and social problems. Mom found herself getting deeply involved in their family matters, especially the girls who found themselves with an unwanted pregnancy. She helped the girls as best she could, intervening between them and their parents, as well as social workers. Mom wanted to make sure the student and the unborn child were protected.

I went about my studies, realizing that soon I would be applying for college and making important career decisions. Mom was helpful and encouraging, always stressing self-confidence and determination while giving me a sense of reality and freedom of choice. She pointed out how hard the real world was and that in order to succeed and be competitive, a good education was imperative. She never pushed me on a career choice, but she did point out the benefits of certain professional fields that were not only financially rewarding but also prestigious and helpful to humanity. She knew I had always expressed a desire for the healing arts and that I was empathetic toward people who were suffering and in need of help. I continued working as an orderly in one of the local hospitals, hoping someday to pursue a career in medicine or dentistry. I found the work interesting and very self-satisfying; it also gave me a sense of independence, knowing I was able to use the money I earned to finance all my social activities with my friends.

The most exciting part of that year was Tony's expected return from the army in February. We were all energized with the prospects of our family once again being together. Mom could now breathe a sigh of relief knowing that her son would soon be home safe and sound. Even though she was proud of her son in the military, she silently worried every day for his safety. I could always see the trepidation in her eyes whenever she read one of his letters or spoke of his travels throughout Europe. Now all her energy was focused on preparing for Tony's homecoming; she planned every detail so his arrival would be extra special and deserving of a king. After all, he was her "numero uno," her number one; the first-born. We were all embroiled in his homecoming, anticipating what new exploits and adventures we as a family would be in store for upon his return. He left home a boy and returned as a man. We were all certain there were many changes all of us would have to adjust to and accept; the biggest change would be his independence and lack of restrictions.

Tony's homecoming was certainly a gala affair replete with presents, wine, a buffet of gourmet Italian delicacies and desserts. Mom went all out for this special and long awaited day. She was so proud of her returning soldier and content to have him back within the family fold. This was truly a day of celebration amongst all the relatives, friends, and neighbors; it lasted until the wee hours of the morning, exhausting all of us. The next day was the beginning of the rest of Tony's new life, one that was to be full of happiness and many rewarding achievements. Mom made sure that Tony had every opportunity and resource to pursue anything he wanted to do. She gave him the backing and security he needed to start a completely new unencumbered life surrounded by supporting and loving parents. Tony chose to work during the day to support his social life and car expenses and go to college at night to finish his education. He was decisively committed to work and school; he now had the maturity and common sense to realize what it took to achieve success in any endeavor.

Mom was so proud of her two sons, both striving for success and advancement in life. She knew all her efforts and sacrifice for her family was paying off in a way that would enhance our lives. She made every moment of our lives seem special and important, always encouraging and supportive. Nothing was too difficult for her to do when it came to her two sons. She was the epitome of a "Mother!"

That spring was the emotional and maturing turning point for Tony; he rekindled his relationship with his first love, Judy. Their romance was no longer long distance between New York and Vermont; Judy moved to New York to work in the city and to be near Tony. She instantly became part of our family, welcomed in with warm and extended arms of love. Mom instinctively assumed the role of mentor and teacher for her son's girlfriend. She knew Judy was far away from home and missed her family. Mom did all she could to lessen her homesickness by including her in all our family affairs. She took her under her wing and treated her like a daughter in every respect. Sunday dinners took on a new manifestation with Judy at the table. Suddenly, the family was growing in new directions and we all were one big happy family. Judy was certainly a beautiful and extraordinary addition to our family; she added a sparkle to our lives.

Mom knew that their romance was headed down the road to a more permanent relationship. Once they were engaged to be married, we all looked forward to the impending marriage with excitement and great expectations. Judy was now an eternal part of our family and would be treated like a daughter by my parents, and a sister by me. Mom and Judy developed a special bond, one of love and mutual respect. The wedding plans consumed much of their time and energy. Mom designed and made Judy's wedding gown with the love and attention to detail that was her forte. It was a project of love; every stitch was sewn with care and finesse, making sure that this was to be a special wedding gown for her son's bride. Every time Judy came over for a fitting, it was a mystery, all of us anticipating how radiant and beautiful she would look on her wedding day. Only Mom and Judy knew what the gown would look like; the rest of the family had to wait for the momentous occasion to view the young bride in her gown.

On September 1, 1962, Tony and Judy exchanged their vows of eternal love in their wedding ceremony at Christ the King church in Rutland, Vermont. It was the first wedding in the family of the new generation of Italian Americans. New hope and great expectations were on the horizon for the new couple as they took on a new and challenging role. It was a great celebration of friends and relatives, lasting for several days. I was the best man, and Judy's sister, Carol, was the maid of honor. As we all expected, Judy looked radiant in her wedding gown. Mom beamed with pride, as this was her special and loving gift to her new daughter. Judy would be the recipient of many more designer fashions as the years progressed; Mom now had a daughter whom she could endow with all her talents as a designer.

Tony and Judy returned from their honeymoon and set up their nest in an apartment in a nearby development. It was the beginning of the rest of their lives together. They both worked toward developing a new and productive life with the expectation of starting a family in the near future. Tony continued his schooling, hoping to be able to advance himself in the business world. During the week, they spent many evenings with us at dinner. Under Mom's tutelage, Judy was taught how to cook all the traditional Italian meals that were passed down from generation to generation. It wasn't long before Judy mastered the art of cooking and carrying on the tradition of Sunday dinner with the family. On many occasions, Judy entertained and fed a crowd of family and relatives in their tiny apartment. The table took up the whole living room and there were wall-to-wall people enjoying the delicacies Judy had learned to prepare so well. Mom was very proud of Judy's accomplishments and how well she carried on the family traditions.

As the seasons passed and holiday traditions continued, we all grew and adapted to the numerous new experiences in our lives. I was engrossed in my college studies, Tony and Judy were planning a family, and Mom and Dad were approaching the pinnacle of their teaching careers. Mom was still involved with the caring and financial responsibilities of her aunts and uncles. She laboriously made the weekly trek into Brooklyn to carry out the many and varied tasks that she had to handle. Mom was very busy all the time, teaching full-time, entertaining and cooking for the family, sewing for Judy, and caring for her elderly relatives. Her energy seemed endless and she never wavered or deviated from her role as wife, mother, teacher, and niece. Her remarkable stamina and dedication to her family and friends were the trademarks of her persona. It was as if her total existence and purpose was to nurture and care for people.

Great and wonderful events happen in all families that are growing. Tony and Judy's life would now take on a new purpose and meaning with the announcement of Judy's pregnancy. We were all jubilant and excited with the news of the impending birth. It was a joyous and happy time in our lives as we all awaited the turning point in our lives; Tony and Judy were to be parents, Mom and Dad were to be grandparents, and I was to be an uncle. We all, in our own way, prepared for our new roles in the expanding family, wondering with great anticipation how each of us would share and interact in the life of the new child. Nothing else seemed to matter in the daily course of our lives at the time; all of our thoughts and energy were focused on the coming of the blessed event.

I was graduating from college and hoping to go on to graduate school to continue my studies. All seemed copasetic as we thought our lives were moving in a positive direction, never thinking anything could alter our happy existence. It was a time for prosperity and the realization of goals and aspirations amongst my generation. Yet, we as a nation were once again embroiled in a war, one that seemed to take on a very critical and unpopular scrutiny in America. The war in Vietnam was now escalating and destroying the lives of many families. As my family prepared for the birth of the new baby, I was notified to report for my induction physical for the Army. Now fear and dismay gripped our family. Mom was once again faced with the ordeal of one of her sons leaving home for the military, but this time going off to war. Her greatest fear was now becoming a reality; her memory of when I was born and how she named me to commemorate the dying soldiers at that time frightened and terrified her. Suddenly, all her joy and happiness over the coming birth of her grandchild was clouded by the doom and gloom of my going off to war.

My fate, like so many other college graduates at the time, was to be drafted into the army and become a commissioned officer in one of the combat branches, a position of leadership and command that would certainly place me in battle. Tony, having had experience in the army and concerned with my welfare, insisted that I forgo my commission and instead enlist into the Army Dental Corps. He felt I would be safer and less apt to be a casualty of war if I were in one of the non-combatant divisions of the army. I listened to his advice and enlisted in the Army Dental Corps for three years, not knowing that it would be a turning point in my future.

Judy gave birth to a baby boy on February 5, 1967, whom they named Anthony, and I left for the army in March. For Mom, it was a bittersweet time; her emotions were tumultuous and vacillating between joy and sadness. I, on the other hand, was not only saddened for having to leave my family at a time when so many joys are shared in a new baby's life, but also fearful of the uncertain prospects of war. My thoughts centered on fulfilling my obligation and performing my duty to my country and hopefully to return home unharmed and unscathed from the ravages of war.

Chapter 8

So Much Missed: So Much More to Experience

The day I left for the army, we had a blizzard in New York and Fort Dix in New Jersey was not accepting new inductees due to the weather conditions. I was sent south, to Georgia; too far for Mom and Dad to visit on Sundays as they did with my brother when he was in basic training. I remembered those Sunday visits when Mom prepared the feasts of plenty for Tony and his friends and how happy he was to be with the family. I missed that during my basic training, which added to my feelings of melancholy and loneliness. Military life during a war carries uncertainties that constantly enter your mind and fill you with apprehension and fear. It took me a long time to adjust to the army and being away from the comforts of home and all the new and exciting things that were happening in my family. Staying in close contact with them by mail enabled me to envision most of what was occurring on the home front. Probably the most missed and nostalgic moments were the family gatherings and the lavish meals Mom had prepared. Army food, while nutritious and plentiful, was mundane as compared to Mom's culinary skills and epicurean talents. Military food was a matter of survival and not a dining experience! My thoughts of real Italian food often left me longing for the "good old days" and what life used to be like.

Unfortunately, during my time in the military, I missed many events that took place at home. I luckily escaped having to be in battle by being stationed in Germany. Being so far away from family and friends was the only real hardship I had to endure. I missed my friends' marriages and births of their children. My friend Richie married Sue shortly before I left for the army, but I did miss seeing Wally's marriage to Holly, the girl I had introduced him to on a grateful blind date when we were in high school. Margie got married, and so did her sister Diana. My cousin Johanna got married and had two boys named John and Peter. Some things can never be recaptured, only lamented.

At home, Mom was well into her role of grandmother, and needless to say, she assumed her new position with all her love and devotion. My nephew was the new center of attention in the family. My father's every waking moment was consumed with his new grandson. Tony and Judy were very fortunate to have Mom and

Dad living so close by, they had built in babysitters. Mom would take care of the baby on most weekends so Tony and Judy could have some free time to be alone or socialize with their friends. Mom knew how important it was for a young couple to be able to have private time together and develop their relationship. Mom also baby-sat when they went away on vacations or company trips. Judy was still the recipient of the latest fashions designed and made by Mom. She was always in style and the envy of all her friends. Mom took pride in seeing Judy look so fashionable and chic in her new outfits, making sure that Judy was always dressed up to date. Every season brought new and numerous garments!

With all the family marriages and births, the holiday meals and family gatherings became enormous in size. Mom was now cooking and serving a multitude of relatives with the same meticulous and gracious style she had done her whole life. The new extended family of in-laws were now exposed to her many culinary skills as well as her hospitable and warm demeanor. No matter whom my mother entertained, she always did it with love and enjoyment; to her it was a matter of pride to be able to cater to and serve her guests in a congenial and graceful way. The new family members were also introduced to the custom of finishing off the sumptuous meals with a glass of *Strega* and toasting to everyone's good health.

Tony's business career was taking off like a wildfire; he was moving up the corporate ladder very rapidly. Promotion after promotion catapulted him to higher and higher management positions. His latest promotion, unfortunately, required him to move to Connecticut, something that he reluctantly had to do in order to remain in the good graces with his superiors. Mom and Dad were devastated over the prospects of having them move and losing the close and warm relationship they were so used to having. Mom knew that it was beneficial to Tony's career to make the move, and she encouraged him to take every opportunity to advance his career. She knew how it was with Dad when he was trying to advance his career, those feelings of uncertainty and desires to become well established and self-reliant. As much as she hated to see Tony, Judy, and the baby leave, she knew it was for the betterment of his career and his future success.

The miles between New York and Connecticut were not an issue; almost every weekend, Mom and Dad would pack up after school on Friday and make the two-hour journey to see "the kids." It became a ritual, sometimes broken up by Tony and Judy coming down for the weekend and staying at Mom's house. Whenever they came down, Mom made sure she had plenty of food as usual and it was always some sort of pasta that Tony loved. The baby never lacked for family involvement or attention; he was growing up in a family that emphasized love and caring and a sense of togetherness. Mom would write to me about their visits, and oh, how I longed to be part of those gatherings and long lavish dinners with stimulating conversations. I knew that my time in the service would soon end and I would once again be part of the family.

Three years was not an eternity, and time does fly by rapidly. Before I knew it, I was making plans to leave Germany, return to the states, and be discharged out of the army. While filled with joy with the prospect of returning to America, I was a little reticent about how I would adjust to being home. I was somewhat of an oddball in a sense; all my friends had careers, wives, houses, and children. I was twenty-six years old, not married, and had no job; I had no idea what the future would hold for me. Returning home as a Vietnam veteran was somewhat of a disadvantage at that time since it was a very unpopular war. Veterans then were not given any special privileges when returning home; in fact, we were treated with disdain and admonishment. It was a disgrace how we were treated; we only did our duty and served our country the best we could. Mom made me feel like a hero on my return; she knew how I felt, and she did everything in her power to build up my self-esteem and self-respect. My homecoming was all I expected it to be: a gala family reunion, complete with Mom's festive expertise.

I felt I had to enter the job force as soon as I could after being discharged. I had to find a way to support myself and be a productive part of society. I really wanted to continue my education with higher degrees, but I was reluctant to go back to school and get my master's degree in psychology. I started my master's degree that summer, but once again, I felt out of place due to my age. I left school shortly after starting and tried the business world. I was not happy and I knew the business world was not for me. Since I had spent three years in the Army Dental Corps and loved the work I did, I contemplated becoming a dentist. Once again, I was faced with the dilemma of how I would support myself and pay for all that schooling. I would have to return to college and take two years of required science courses to enable me to gain entrance into a dental school, and then spend four years in dental school. It seemed almost insurmountable and overwhelming to me. Mom, as usual, gave me the encouragement and support to motivate me to follow my vision—she was very familiar with changing careers at a later age. Mom and Dad pledged their support both financially and emotionally.

Tony and Judy moved again to another part of Connecticut and Judy gave birth to a beautiful baby girl on May 13, 1970, whom they named Denise. Once again, the baby was the center of attention, and for Mom, it was a special joy because she now had another girl in the family whom she could shower with her designing skills. Mom went all out making outfits for Denise, making sure she was the best-dressed little princess in the neighborhood. She was really a beautiful and petite little girl with all the fire and energy of a volcano. Tony often referred to Denise as his "entertainment center." Two years later, another promotion for Tony required another move, but this time it was back to New York, much to the delight of everyone. Now the family was once again together and in closer proximity.

I started school and worked at night to help support myself and lessen my parents' financial burden.

While in school, I hastily entered into a relationship and got married. It would later prove to be a mistake and end in divorce later on in life. Nonetheless, I juggled dental school and a new marriage, and was able to successfully finish my schooling at Emory University Dental School in 1976 at the age of thirty-two. It was a late start as a professional, but as the expression goes, "It's never too late." I opened up a practice in my old neighborhood with the help of Mom and Dad. Once again, Mom was there with her words of encouragement and unending support.

Mom and Dad had retired after both having spent very successful careers in teaching. They reaped the rewards of many years of hard work and dedication by spending their retirement years between New York and Vermont; something they had planned and saved for their whole lives. Mom still entertained the family and friends with lavish feasts both in New York and in Vermont. She had a lot more free time now that she was not teaching, but she was never idle; her days were filled with sewing, cooking, and very often being with her grandchildren. Anthony and Denise spent many weeks in Vermont during the summer under Mom's watchful eye and supervision, much the same as Tony and I had experienced during our summer months. They, however, were much more fortunate than Tony and I were when we were their age. Mom and Dad were more financially secure during this stage of their lives and were able to shower their grandchildren with many elaborate and expensive playthings. Their time spent in

Vermont was filled with many memorable experiences not afforded to many children of their era.

Tony and Judy benefited from their children spending time in Vermont too; they were free to spend time alone without the children to travel and enjoy time with their close friends Bob and Carolee, and Bill and Patty. Mom was the consummate babysitter on many occasions, especially on weekends in New York. Judy was able to accompany Tony on many business trips and vacations while Mom babysat, giving her and Tony the peace of mind that their children were well cared for and secure. Mom often volunteered to take care of the children even if they had no place to travel, just to allow them to have some time alone together as a couple. Everyone benefited from Mom's generosity; she was always giving of herself in a loving and unselfish manner.

Mom still attended to the needs of her aged aunts and uncles and was unyielding in her caring for them. As time progressed, she fulfilled her reverent duties as they became ill and passed away. She made sure that they all had dignified and religious funeral services. Mom was a wonderful and caring niece and her love and respect for her elders was always exalted to them. She never wavered in her caring or respect for her family.

We all spent a lot of time together as a family; Mom was the cohesive factor that always brought us together, either for a Sunday dinner or a holiday gathering. No matter what the occasion, it was always a festive treat to be together and share Mom's elaborate meals. She always planed a meal around everyone's likes and desires. She made sure that each one of us enjoyed a special favorite entree. You could see the joy in her face as we all energetically consumed her special meals; nothing gave her more pleasure than to please her family. Mom took pride in everything she did, and making her family happy was her biggest joy in life and special gift to us; we were her priority. Our expanded families and all their relatives were also the lucky recipients of Mom's gracious and multifaceted talents and love. It was always a highly anticipated and joyous occasion to be invited to Mom's "table of love."

Mom and Dad grew old very gracefully and they seemed almost ageless for a long period. Age was never a hindering factor with Mom's ability to entertain or share her time with her family. When Mom was well into her eighties, there were many times when Judy and Denise would accompany her into Manhattan on a shopping spree and they would both return exhausted from trying to keep up with her energetic pace and cavorting in and out of the stores. Mom always felt that age was a mental state of mind and not a physical one—she was a proponent of the saying, "You are as old as you feel." She always had prid in herself and in her appearance and never gave into being dowdy or decrepit in her style of dress or how she carried herself. Her fashion background and experience always manifested itself in how she presented herself. We all always admired her and were proud of her appearance. She was designing and making clothes in her mid-eighties with the same energy and vitality as she had as a young designer.

The so-called "Golden Years" are not always replete with joy and happiness. While Mom and Dad were fortunate to have reached well into their eighties and still enjoyed retirement, their brothers and sisters were not so fortunate. They, as well as their spouses, passed away in their early eighties. Octogenarians start feeling the loneliness and isolation when all their family is gone and they are the lone survivors. Sadness and death escapes no family; it's the ones who remain who feel the pain and loss. Mom was very close to her sister and she felt her loss deeply. Death at an older age is presumably expected and an inevitable event in life. Sometimes death is untimely, as in the case of my cousin Louis. He passed away in his early fifties from lymphoma. His early passing was mourned by all of us and extremely difficult for my cousin Johanna to accept. I was very close to Louis and I will always cherish the memories of our special times together. While all the losses sadden families, the growth and development of new children somehow ameliorate the feelings associated with the passing of loved ones.

As the years passed, Mom and Dad started to show their advanced years, but they remained fairly independent and self-sufficient. I became more and more involved in their daily lives as I recognized a need to help them with certain routine tasks that became too burdensome for them to handle on their own. Since Dad was no longer able to drive, I often took them to church and dinners at Tony and Judy's home. I became involved in managing their financial affairs and making sure all the bills were paid and their investments properly maintained. Dad was always good at managing his finances with pen and paper; when I took over the finances and computerized them, it confused him, but at the same time, relieved him of the arduous and time-consuming burden. My daily visits were spent helping them organize their lives and making things as easy and simple as possible. It was fortuitous for them that my office was a few blocks away and I was able to walk over and always be readily available for them. I know it gave them great comfort and security knowing I was so close by. I enjoyed helping them and tending to their needs; it gave me a great feeling of satisfaction to be able to take care of my parents who were always so loving and caring to me.

I could sense my Dad's frustration as he had to relinquish more and more of his duties as man of the house to me. Mom also had to kind of take over with most of the decision-making responsibilities. She still maintained a sharpness and aptitude to comprehend many important household affairs. Mom became more and more dependent on me as the years passed; she wanted to make sure that her decisions were supported by me, so as not to usurp Dad's presumed control of the household. Her role as homemaker never wavered; she continued to cook and maintain the house with some help from a housekeeper who came once a week to clean. Mom still did most of the grocery shopping in the local stores on a daily basis. The daily meals during the week were simple and routine; she made sure that they both ate healthy and nutritious meals. She still prepared many Sunday dinners for all of us to enjoy in a more elaborate style, but with more exertion and effort. I could see that she was also slowing down, yet she wanted to continue to please her family. She still served the meals with grace and style, always taking pride in her presentation. There was always plenty of food, and Mom made sure it was always one of our favorite Italian meals. She still took great pride and joy in serving us *Strega* at the end of the meal. She would always have a big smile on her face as she sipped her drink and would recant her childhood memories. She was always an ardent storyteller and would repeat many of her adventures and escapades to us at the dinner table. Even though we heard the stories numerous times, we still gave her the attention and respect by listening with interest. Dad, on the other hand, would often admonish Mom for being so repetitive. Those stories are imbedded in my mind and I am sure in the rest of my family's minds as well.

I began to spend more and more time with Mom and Dad during the late spring of 1997. My increased time with them was motivated by a deteriorating marriage and the time spent away from home was needed. I also spent a lot of time with Tony and Judy on weekends; we would often go to visit my nephew, who now was living in Connecticut. They were all very supportive and loving in allowing me time to vent my feelings and my frustrations about a very difficult and emotional time in my life. Mom, most of all, was the stoic and encouraging pillar of strength. Her years of wisdom and common sense were a great source of comfort and solace. Mom was always able to be the peacemaker in the family, having had to deal with many emotional and difficult decisions her whole life; her experience and manner were a blessing to say the least. She was never prejudicial or cruel; she would always try to find some good in every situation no matter how unpleasant the circumstances presented themselves. She knew that I was suffering and she made every attempt to support and encourage me. Her love and understanding helped me to overcome my feelings of helplessness and confusion. Mothers have a special way of easing the pain that their children are going through.

Not all was unpleasant during that time of year. We celebrated Dad turning ninety years old in July and Mom turning ninety in September. It was certainly something to celebrate; Tony and I felt very fortunate to have both parents alive and with us at such an old age. Mom was very proud to have achieved such a milestone in life and was very grateful for her good health and keen senses and alert mind. Physically, she was the epitome of health; all systems working well and no signs of debilitation. Dad, on the other hand, really started to show his advanced years. He was not very accepting of his frailties and declining health. His once jovial and outgoing personality changed to one of somber and gloom. He became more and more reclusive and disinterested in the simple pleasures of life. It upset Mom to see her once vibrant and strong husband so morose and demoralized. She, nonetheless, stood by and catered to his needs like a dutiful wife. She made sure that he had three healthy meals a day and that he took his prescribed medications on time. Mom was the chief cook and bottle washer so to speak. She tried to make sure that he had some physical activity and did not just sit all day. She would often send him to the store to pick up a household item so he would get some exercise and possibly interact with some neighbors along the way.

It was very apparent that Dad's care and constant supervision was taking a toll on Mom both physically and mentally. I did whatever I could to intervene and lessen Mom's burden. Most nights I would have dinner with them and try to add some distraction to the doleful and humdrum surroundings. My presence was supportive of Mom and gave her a little diversification in her daily routine. Dad was not too receptive to change his routine; even though I was there, he would not deviate from his ritualistic behavior of early dinner, brief viewing of television, and early bedtime. When Dad went to bed, I remained for a few hours to listen to Mom and let her vent her feelings or just chat about trivial matters. Even though Mom was going through a sad and difficult time taking care of Dad, she still took the time to listen to my woes and anguish. Our conversations at night were mutually supportive and helpful. I would leave their house somewhat tranquil and calm.

Dad's health was becoming more and more of a concern for all of us. He became very weak and was unable to climb the stairs up to his bedroom. We decided to convert the downstairs den into a bedroom for him. We ordered a hospital bed and moved the furniture around to accommodate the new living circumstances. Mom was reluctant to leave Dad downstairs alone while she slept in her room upstairs, but we insisted that he would be fine since the hospital bed came equipped with side rails. The day the hospital bed arrived, I made sure that I was there to help Dad with the psychological adjustment of needing to remain on one floor and dealing with yet one more frailty of aging. Dinner that night was somewhat silent, with slight interjections of how it would be easier for Dad to be living on one floor. I made sure Dad was settled in his new bed before leaving for the evening. I told him I loved him and gave him a kiss on his forehead. He seemed very comfortable and drifted off to sleep easily. Mom and I were relieved to know how fast he adapted to his new routine of sleeping in a bed with protective rails. Mom and I spoke for a short while and then I left her to tend to her last minute chores before retiring herself.

Chapter 9

Emptiness and Loss: The Reversal of Care

I returned home late that evening after leaving Dad in his new sleeping environment somewhat saddened, yet confident that he would be safe and comfortable. I lay awake for some time thinking about how vibrant and strong Dad used to be. The once energized and athletic man who worked day and night and was the center of attention at parties and social events was now reduced to a frail and weak old man. Now rather than dominating a situation or conversation, he hovered in a corner and was uncommunicative and silent. The consummate jokester was now morose and depressed. I not only felt sad to see him like that, but I knew that he himself realized that the spark of life was gone and that he was near the end. My thoughts also drifted to Mom, and how for sixty-three years of marriage, she had stood by her husband through thick and thin, and now had to deal with an even more heartrending chapter in their lives. I slowly drifted off to a restless and labored sleep. In the darkness and silence of the night, I could hear my heart beating; the rhythm somehow lulled me into a deeper and more relaxed sleep.

The telephone rang in the darkness and startled me out of a short but deep sleep. I glanced at the bedside clock and noticed it was 2 a.m. . I answered the phone and heard Mom on the other end in a hysterical and frantic voice tell me that Dad was acting erratically and trying to get out of the hospital bed. I told her I would be right over. I quickly dressed and drove to their house and found Dad very agitated and incoherent. He had one leg out of the bed rail and was shaking the rail in an attempt to get out of bed. I quickly placed his leg back in bed and attempted to calm him down. He had apparently awakened during the night and was confused by his surroundings. He was fearful that he was in the hospital and all alone. I reassured him that he was at home, that Mom and I were there with him, that he was safe and secure, and that there was no reason to be frightened. I quieted him down and stroked his head as he slowly drifted back to sleep. Mom was still agitated and crying. I gave her a sedative and had her lay down on the sofa in the living room, reassuring her that I would sleep on the couch in the den with Dad and monitor his condition. After getting Mom settled down and confident that I was there to help her, I went into the den, sat up, and observed Dad as he slept. He appeared to be in a very light and restless sleep, softly muttering incoherent sounds as if he were dreaming. I dozed off in the chair somewhere around 5 a.m. only to be awakened by louder sounds coming from Dad. I rushed to his side and noticed his breathing was labored and I was unable to get him to respond to my voice. I kept calling out to him as I stroked his clammy and warm forehead. I realized that there was more going on than agitation and confusion. I called 911 and had an ambulance dispatched to the house. Mom, in the meantime, had awakened and I quickly ushered her into the kitchen and assured her that everything was all right. I called Diana next door and asked her to come over and stay with Mom in the kitchen. I then called Judy, informed her of the situation, and asked her to contact Tony at work. I hung up the phone and went back into the den to check on Dad. He was still moaning slightly and his breathing and pulse were weak. I kissed him on the forehead and reassured him everything would be okay and that help was on the way.

Dad died moments before the ambulance arrived, sending a deep shiver throughout my body. I froze for a moment, not realizing what had just happened. The man who emigrated to the United States at the age of three, educated himself, married my mother, and gave rise to three generations of new world Americans had left this world. The patriarch of our family was no longer here to see the family he created flourish, prosper, and enjoy the culmination of his dreams. Reality quickly set in and I knew that I was now faced with the heart-rending task of telling Mom that Dad had passed away. I went into the kitchen and took Diana aside and quietly told her that Dad was gone. We had Mom sit down as I broke the news to her as gently and softly as I could. She wanted to see Dad; I took her to his bedside and she leaned over and sweetly kissed him on the forehead and touched his hand in a tender and loving manner. I held her in my arms as she quietly sobbed. I reassured her that Dad was at peace now and in the arms of the Lord.

Judy arrived shortly after to discover the course of events that had transpired. She was visibly shaken and upset. She quickly went to Mom and tried to comfort her, realizing that she had to gather her strength to help Mom cope with Dad's passing. Tony arrived about an hour later, having abruptly left a business meeting in New Jersey. He went into the den and spent a few quiet moments with Dad; Tony's anguish and heartbreak were evident as he came to Mom's side. We all realized the reality of the moment, but what was foremost in our minds and hearts now was standing by Mom and supporting her through the days to follow. Our hearts were broken, but we had to muster up the strength and fortitude to get through this difficult period in our lives. The rest of the day was spent contacting Dad's doctor and making arrangements with the funeral home. Judy and I accompanied Mom to the funeral home to make the final arrangement for Dad, while Tony was assigned the difficult task of calling all the friends and family and informing them of Dad's passing. Mom, once again, went about the process of making Dad's burial arrangements with the same strength and stoic fortitude as she had done so many other times for family members in the past. She somehow gathered the strength to be able to realize that this was the reality of life and it was time for her to act and not react. Her whole life had been ruled by "taking the bull by the horns" and now was not the time to portray weakness and indecision, but a time to act and clearly make the right decisions. There was a time for grieving and a time for acting; Mom was able to separate the two and place them in the proper perspective.

Mom was always level-headed and planned ahead for many important things in life. Growing up at the turn of the century and living through the Depression gave her a sense of what was important and what priority certain things should have. Many years ago, she had purchased burial crypts in the mausoleum at St. John's cemetery. She knew from experience that visiting loved ones buried in a cemetery during inclement weather and cold winters was somewhat of a burden on family members. She and Dad always visited their parents and relatives at the cemetery and maintained the gravesites with flowering plants. She wanted to spare her children the burden of having to take care of their graves and be exposed to the cold and rainy weather. Mom was always thinking of other people, even planning after her death to make them comfortable.

The next two days were spent at the wake for Dad at the funeral home. There was a crowd of people day and night coming by to pay their respects to Mom and the rest of the family. Dad had been very popular in the community and had touched many people's lives in a positive way. It was a very emotionally exhausting few days for all of us, especially Mom. She held up very well for a ninety-year-old woman, never giving in to any frailties or emotional outbreaks. She held herself together with all the grace and charm she had always displayed her whole life. She greeted each and every visitor at the funeral home with a warm and cordial smile, and thanked them for their attendance. The funeral services at our church culminated with Dad's burial at the cemetery. We all said our last good-byes to Dad and departed for a luncheon for the family and friends who attended the services. That evening back at the house we all toasted to Dad with a glass of *Strega*.

The next day, all of the out-of-town relatives left and Mom was left all alone. Dad's death and the thought of Mom being suddenly left on her own was the impetus for me to make a long and overdue decision. I had been procrastinating about leaving my wife and putting an end to my unhappy home environment; I collected my thoughts and realized what I had to do. I left my wife and home and moved in with Mom. I knew that at least I would be in familiar surroundings, being in the home in which I was born and raised, and that I would be somewhat of a comfort to Mom during her period of mourning. Part of my indecision about separating was the fear of where I would go or how I would live. It was very reassuring to know I had a place to go to that was comfortable and full of love. Many men are faced with the same fears and are left out in the cold to fend for themselves at a later stage in life. The breakup of a marriage is never pleasant and the sudden changes that accompany divorce are overwhelming and often times catastrophic. I was fortunate to have a place to go to and heal my wounds.

As much as I thought I was to be a comfort to Mom, it was she that was a comfort to me. She realized how hard it was for me and she empathized with the anguish I was going through. Even though she was going through her own period of adjustment and dealing with her loss, she found the time to be consoling and encouraging to me. As always, she had profound words of wisdom and put a positive spin on my misgivings. She never wavered from being strong and positive; her encouragement and support was endless. In a way, my situation was good for Mom; it helped take her mind off her own suffering and gave her a new purpose. Mothers really are made in heaven!

I continued my daily routine of working at my office and running my practice. After work, I would return home and be greeted by Mom and the wonderful meals she prepared. It was very comforting to know that at the end of a workday, you were being treated to a wonderful and sumptuous meal. Mom knew how much I appreciated her cooking; she made sure she prepared all my favorite meals. It seemed as if she were invigorated by preparing these meals. As usual, Mom took pride and joy in presenting a feast of a meal. After dinner, we would talk and she would reminisce over all her experiences. She also took time and the interest in what was happening in my career and personal life. We fed off each other, one encouraging the other. Mom was a great listener as well as a great storyteller; she had the ability to tell a story and bring relevance to a current situation. Some evenings we spent hours just talking, then she would go to bed and I would stay up and watch TV for a while. Those nights of long conversations were very comforting to me and helped ease my uncertainties and doubts about my life and myself.

During the week, our routine was the same: work, dinner conversation, TV, sleep. On the weekend, we often went to Tony and Judy's for Sunday dinner. It was a pleasant break for both of us, and it was a treat to spend time together as a family. Judy always prepared one of Mom's favorite dishes that were a delight to all of us. We all felt the absence of Dad, but as time went on we all adjusted to the reality of his passing and took joy in the fact that we were still a family enjoying the gifts God had given us. The reality of life is that life goes on and you have to grasp each and every moment of happiness and be thankful for all that we have. Tony and Judy did all they could to make our visits pleasant and comfortable. As much as Mom enjoyed getting out and going to Tony and Judy's for dinner, she was always happy to return home and be in her own house. She always referred to her home as her palace. When you reach a certain age, there is a tremendous security in being in your own familiar surroundings. Mom's palace was her comfort zone!

I also tried to break up the weekly routine with Mom by treating her to a few nights out to dinner. She loved to get dressed up and go out to dinner at one of the local restaurants. One restaurant in particular was her favorite, Dante's Restaurant, a local Italian restaurant that had been in the neighborhood for over fifty years. It had a warm and cozy atmosphere, and the food was real homemade, old-world Italian. Mom felt very at home there, and the owners made her feel very special. It was a family-run business and they always made you feel like you were part of their family. Pat, the owner, along with her sister, Norma, who was the manager, and Peter, her son, who was the chef, and his sister, Karla, who was the co-manager and bartender, made you feel that you were dining in their home. They always made a fuss over Mom and were always entertained by her stories from her vast experiences. Whenever I suggested to Mom that we go out for dinner and I told her we were going to Dante's, her eyes would light up and a big smile would cross her face. I enjoyed taking Mom out and having her be treated like a queen so much. She always enjoyed her dinner, and especially the homemade desserts!

The days went fast, but the nights seemed to drag on for me. I was engrossed in all the legal and financial complications that were the bitter reality that comes with separation and divorce. Mom seemed to be adjusting to her new position in life as a widow better than I was as a newly-single male. Even though I found great emotional comfort living in Mom's house and having shelter and company, there was still an emptiness and loneliness that gripped at me deep inside. Mom sensed my feelings and knew that they were more than just the anguish and grief of divorce. She had suggested one evening after dinner that I stop by one of the local restaurant/pubs in the area, which was very familiar to me in the neighborhood. The Sly Fox Inn was directly across from my office and I knew the owner, Joe, very well. I would often have lunch there and occasionally took Mom there for dinner. It was only two blocks from our house and within walking distance.

That evening, after dinner, I took Mom's suggestion and decided to walk over to the Sly Fox and spend a few hours out for a change of pace. I assured Mom I would be home before she went to bed. I wanted to make sure she felt secure and unafraid knowing I was home before she went to sleep. I was not accustomed to going out at night and spending time at a local pub; I felt awkward and uneasy. I arrived there while happy hour was still in progress, sat at the bar, and looked around for a familiar face. Joe came over to me and we exchanged congenialities. He was glad to see me and we began to talk about trivial matters and exchanged a few jokes throughout our conversation. As more and more people arrived, Joe had to greet them and be hospitable. Some of the people were playing darts and others were just talking and laughing. The atmosphere was filled with levity and merriment; everyone was in high spirits and having a good time. I remained in the background and just watched and observed. I was still in a quiet and doleful mood.

It wasn't long after I had arrived at the Sly Fox that I noticed an individual walk in and saw that his presence immediately commanded attention. Everyone seemed to know him and all at once, the laughter and frolicking became louder. It resembled an episode out of the well-known TV show *Cheers*. His voice rose above all others and his laughter filled the room with a contagious cheerfulness. I just watched and listened to him and his joking and skillful repartee. I noticed that Joe was very friendly with him as they engaged in light conversation. Joe motioned for me to come over to where they were standing, and I was introduced to him. His name was Danny, a former New York City homicide detective. He was a giant of a man, towering over me like a mighty oak tree. While listening to him speak and joke around, a smile immediately appeared on my face; his humorous and jovial demeanor captivated me. Danny certainly had the propensity to command attention and the talent to make everyone laugh. I left after a few hours and walked home, realizing that I still had a smile on my face and was feeling very relaxed. Mom was sitting up watching television; I sat down to join her and as we began to converse, I described the humorous events of the evening. She was pleased that I had a good time and she remarked how relaxed and cheerful I appeared.

As time progressed, my evening visits to the Sly Fox became more and more of a routine. I found it to be very comforting and calming, and it definitely elevated my spirits. Every time I walked over there, a smile appeared on my face when I spotted Danny's car parked outside; I instantly knew I was in for an evening of laughter. I developed a wonderful and meaningful friendship with Danny and grew to know that beneath his giant stature and tough exterior was a heart of gold and a loyal and devoted friend. He was responsible for changing my life around from one of sadness and self-pity to one of joviality and fun. Everyone in my family noticed the change in my personality and mood since I met Danny. Mom was especially happy that I found a good friend and that I was starting to enjoy myself again.

Mom was also starting to show signs of her mood and spirits being elevated, partially because I was in better spirits, and partly due to her acceptance of the big changes in her life as a widow. She wasn't jumping from the rafters, but she definitely seemed more content and at ease. I know she felt secure in her own home and felt safe knowing she was not alone. She also felt proud that she could still cook and serve meals that were special traditional favorites of mine. Mom always took pride in her cooking and she felt that it was necessary to continue with her family traditions. For me, it was wonderful to come home to such great meals and share them with her.

Winter was approaching and Christmas was right around the corner. Even though it was common for a respectable period of mourning after losing your husband, Mom felt that we should still in some way celebrate the holidays. She felt that Dad would have wanted her and us as a family to carry on with the old world Italian traditional Christmas Eve dinner. This particular holiday meal required a tremendous amount of preparation and planning. It was a little too much for Mom to handle by herself. Luckily, Judy was familiar with all the work and attention to detail that this meal required, since she had prepared it many times with Mom.

Now that the family had grown and my nephew, Anthony, and his wife, Amy, were living in Connecticut with their new son, Palmer, it was decided that we would celebrate the holidays with them in their home. It was a lot easier for Mom, me, Tony, and Judy to travel to Connecticut rather than having Anthony and Amy lug all the paraphernalia associated with a young child down to New York. Amy's mother and father, as well as her sister, were also celebrating the holidays with us. Overall, it made sense for us to travel; however, Mom was a little reluctant due to the ice and snow on the roads that is usually prevalent at that time of the year. We all reassured her it would be safe and that we would be careful while driving.

The week prior to our journey to Connecticut was filled with shopping for presents and preparing all the special delicacies for the holiday meal. Judy was responsible for making certain dishes and Mom handled the rest. It was very time-consuming and attention to detail was of the utmost importance. The only difficulty that Mom anticipated was cooking all the food with Judy in a strange kitchen. Mom and Judy solved that problem partially by making sure that they packed an assortment of large pots and pans that were necessary to cook the array of foods to be served. They also made sure they brought plenty of spices and herbs that were the necessary extra ingredients that enhanced the special flavors that were unique to the Italian cuisine. When all was said and done, our journey looked like a caravan of food being shipped to Italy. Mom was excited in a way, knowing that Amy's family was added to the list of friends and family about to partake in her culinary delights and become part of our Italian tradition. By the way, we also packed a bottle of *Strega* to make sure the meal was complete.

Chapter 10

The Fall: Fear, Determination

Our journey on Christmas Eve day was quite challenging due to the heavy holiday traffic and inclement weather. The snow flurries and foggy conditions necessitated slower speeds, making it a tense trip. Mom sat quietly in the passenger seat all the way, but I could sense her nervousness. I made sure I drove slowly and cautiously to make her feel more at ease. Mom never really liked long drives, especially during bad weather. She managed to survive the trip well, and when we arrived, she thanked God for our safe trip. Tony and Judy had arrived about one hour earlier; he had often been referred to as the Mario Andretti driver in the family. I, on the other hand, chose to be more conservative and considerate of Mom's fears and apprehension.

Mom and I were glad to have finished our trip and felt comfortable and cozy in Anthony and Amy's home. The house was replete with colorful Christmas decorations and the fireplace gave a special warm and inviting feeling to their home; even their dog, Chiro, wore a red ribbon around her neck. It was snowing lightly outside, making it a very charming and picturesque setting. It was a happy house full of people filled with merriment and the holiday spirit. It was early afternoon and we had a few hours before we had to start cooking all the food we brought from New York. Everything was prepared ahead of time and most of the items had to be only heated; the spaghetti sauce was made and the shrimp was already breaded.

Since Amy's parents and sister had been staying at the house after arriving from Iowa earlier that week, Mom and I and Tony and Judy had made arrangements to sleep at one of the local motels in town. We had reservations, but had not yet checked in. Tony and I decided to drive over to the motel to check in and unload the luggage to avoid the hustle and bustle later on that evening. Judy wanted to come with us to unpack her clothes and check on the accommodations; Mom, for some unknown reason, wanted to join us. We felt there was no reason for her to leave the warm and comfortable environment and go out into the cold just to check into the motel with us, but she was insistent. We decided to exit the house through the garage; it was easier than trekking through the snow to the cars from the front entrance. We all proceeded to leave through the back entrance down a short flight of stairs to the garage.

Mom was descending the stairs, and miscalculated the last step. Within a split second, she was flat on her face at the bottom of the stairs. Panic set in and we all ran to her side. She was shaking like a leaf in the wind, dazed and frightened. She did not seem to be in pain and there was no visible sign of bleeding. At the age of ninety, any fall should be considered serious and due caution should be exercised when trying to move a person. She calmed down and regained her composure, but was still somewhat frightened. We gently lifted her and placed her sitting in a chair; her only complaint was a slight pain in her upper right leg. We carried her back up the stairs and into the house and gave her a drink of water. My biggest fear, which was very common for someone her age, was that she had broken her hip.

Luckily, one of my nephew's neighbors had a wheelchair leftover from when his mother-in-law had lived with him. We sat Mom in the wheelchair and made her as comfortable as possible. She was not complaining of any severe pain, but I could sense she was not herself. She said she was sore and her leg hurt when she tried to move it. Everyone was concerned, but expressed doubt that she had broken anything. I, on the other hand, had this deep concern that she could have fractured her leg or worse yet, her hip. Everyone told me I was overreacting and should not alarm Mom with my suspicions.

Somehow, we managed to salvage the rest of the holiday evening we were so looking forward to celebrating. Judy, with the help of all of us, managed to serve the traditional Christmas Eve dinner. We all enjoyed the meal, but we were all very sad to see Mom in such an incapacitated state. Mom just sat there and ate very little. I could tell by her eyes that she was in more pain than what she led us to believe. Somehow, I felt Mom wanted us all to enjoy the evening and not worry about her. She managed to partake in family conversation, but not in her usual manner. There were no long familiar and repetitive stories, as she was so famous for telling. It seemed that she just tried to be sociable without commanding center stage. The only thing that seemed to bring a glimmer of a smile to her face was when we toasted to everyone's health with a glass of *Strega*.

We put Mom to bed early that evening; to say the least, she had a grueling and exhausting day. Amy's sister, Ann, who was a nurse, and her mother, Jean, were like angels of mercy. They attended to Mom's needs throughout the night, helping her undress, and waking during the night to take her to the bathroom. They were both very loving and caring. Mom spent somewhat of a comfortable night, not really in pain, just a little sore and achy. The next morning we placed Mom back in the wheelchair so as not to have her strain her leg. We all celebrated Christmas day with another wonderful meal and mainly rested nice and cozy by the warmth of the fireplace. Still, in the back of my mind, I was concerned about Mom. We had originally planned to stay in Connecticut for a few days and make it a nice long holiday visit. I insisted that the next day we take Mom for an x-ray of her right hip and leg as a precautionary measure to rule out any possibility of a fracture. Everyone still thought I was overreacting, but heeded my wishes.

The next morning, we transported Mom very cautiously and carefully to an x-ray clinic nearby in town. I could tell Mom was very apprehensive and frightened. I tried to reassure her that there was nothing to worry about and that this was just a precautionary measure. I was certain that in Mom's mind, she was remembering how her sister suffered when she broke her hip and the long and arduous rehabilitation she had to endure. Once the technician wheeled Mom into the x-ray room, all kind of thoughts ran wildly through my mind also. I had to maintain an aura of calm and compose myself if I were to be of any help to Mom. I tried to collect my thoughts and think of how best to deal with whatever the outcome may be.

The radiologist came into the waiting room and presented us with the bad news that I had feared all along. Mom had a fracture of the right hip. Needless to say, we were all very upset and concerned for Mom's safety and welfare. Now was not the time to react, but to act; something Mom herself had always preached and lived by. We collectively decided that to admit Mom in a hospital in Connecticut would prove to be out of the question. It was more practical for Mom to be in a New York hospital near us so that we would be able to monitor her care and comfort her. The radiologist assured us that transporting her to New York in my car would not cause her any further injury or endanger her in any way as long as she was immobile. We placed her ever so gently in the front passenger seat of my car and reclined the seat back as far as it would go. Mom was silent, yet pensive. I explained to her exactly what the doctor said and that she had to have her hip operated on so she could get better. I assured her that she would be fine and as good as new in a few weeks. It broke my heart to see her so distraught and fearful. She was now vulnerable and weak, something I have never seen in my mother. I knew it was time for me to take control of the situation and make sure that she was well taken care of and secure.

From the car, I phoned a friend of mine who was an orthopedic surgeon on staff at St. Joseph's hospital in Queens. I explained the situation to him and he reassured me that he would meet us at the hospital and that he would give Mom the best of care. Mom seemed to relax a little more knowing that a friend of mine was going to take care of her. She trusted me implicitly and knew that her best interests were of my utmost concern. The drive back to New York seemed endless; thankfully, it was a smooth and uneventful journey. Mom managed to doze off to sleep for a good portion of the trip; no doubt, she was physically and emotionally exhausted. As much as I tried to concentrate on driving, all sorts of thoughts were racing through my mind. I was fearful that Mom would not be able to walk again and that she would be confined to a wheelchair like so many people her age. I know Mom would have a hard time dealing with being an invalid; she has always been a strong and self-sufficient woman. She was always the caretaker of others and now she was facing the grim reality of her own possible dependence on others. Her whole existence, from childhood until now, had been one of the custodian of people's fate, and now she would have to be the one who was weak and defenseless and at the mercy of others.

We arrived at the hospital's emergency entrance around mid-afternoon. My friend Tony met us there as promised. He ordered more x-rays of Mom's hip so he could better evaluate her condition and plan what type of surgery she would need. After reading the x-rays, he informed us that he would have to put a screw in her hip to close the fracture and stabilize her hip. He scheduled the surgery for early the next morning. Mom was promptly admitted and a series of blood tests were obtained for screening purposes. We assured Mom that everything would be all right and that she was safe and in competent hands. She seemed to be receptive and accepting to the idea of having surgery. She did, however, voice her concerns about the recuperative aspects of the procedure. We jokingly told her she would be up and running in a few days. She smiled and gave us one of her cunning little half smiles that indicated she knew better.

After she was settled in her room for the evening, we felt it better to leave and let her get a well-needed and restful night of sleep. We kissed her good-bye and told her we would see her bright and early the next morning. She appeared to be relaxed, but she did show a faint sign of being afraid to be left alone. We put the television on to help lull her to sleep. Once we were certain that she was resting comfortably, we left the hospital to go grab something to eat. It was late and we were exhausted and worn out from the long trip and the tensions surrounding the whole day's events.

After dinner, Tony and Judy went home to Merrick and I went back to Mom's house. It was a very eerie feeling, entering the house without Mom being there; it seemed so empty, cold, and unnatural for Mom not to be there. Her presence always gave a warmth and fullness to the house. I felt sort of awkward and uneasy there all by myself, alone and quiet, the silence filled the air with an ominous feeling of desolation and emptiness. I turned on the television to break the silence and to help pass the time. Completely exhausted and emotionally drained, I fell quickly asleep in the recliner while watching television in the den. The next morning I awoke somewhat refreshed, but the emptiness and silence was still there, making me feel sad and alone. I quickly freshened up and left to meet Tony and Judy at the hospital.

When we went to her room, we were surprised to find out that Mom had already been operated on and was doing well in the recovery room. The surgeon informed us that the operation went well and that Mom was resting comfortably and that she would be back in her room shortly. We breathed a sigh of relief and relaxed as we thought the worst was over and that she tolerated the surgery without any complications. At Mom's age, a multitude of adverse reactions could occur undergoing anesthesia as well as the surgical procedure itself. Now what was foremost in our minds was her healing and recuperation period. There were so many yet unanswered questions that we had regarding her condition and what was to be expected during the next few days and weeks ahead. I, in particular, had many questions and concerns because I knew I was the one living with Mom, and ultimately the one who would be responsible for her care and well-being.

After a few hours, Mom was brought back to her room. We greeted her with big smiles on our faces and with hugs and kisses. She was very groggy and disoriented; no doubt, still feeling the lingering effects of the anesthesia. She was not very communicative; she just laid there in her bed, motionless and silent with her eyes closed. Every once in a while she would open her eyes and respond with a soft and gentle smile. She appeared to be comfortable and not in pain, but she looked so pathetic and fragile just lying there. The nurse reassured us that her condition was very common for her age and she suggested to us that we leave and let her rest for a few more hours and that when we returned she would be more alert and responsive. We heeded her advice and left to have some lunch at a nearby diner. I was relieved to know that Mom was resting and free of pain. Even though the nurse reassured us that Mom would be fine in a few hours, I was still concerned and somewhat skeptical about Mom's delayed recovery and prolonged unresponsiveness.

When we returned from lunch, we found Mom awake and sitting up in bed. She turned her head toward us as we walked into the room, but she had a blank stare in her eyes, as if she was wondering who we were. I went over to her and kissed her on the cheek, and as I bent over to her, she reached for my face with her hand and was waving it back and forth. She said she was cleaning cobwebs from my face. She had a very determined look in her eyes as if it was a task she had to perform. Mom was totally oblivious to our presence, other than her determination to clear my face. We realized at that point that she was still feeling the post-operative hallucinogenic effects of the anesthesia. The nurse once again reassured us that her behavior was normal for her age, that we should let her rest the remainder of the day, and that she would be greatly improved tomorrow. We left the hospital hoping that tomorrow would bring a better day.

The next few days proved to be very disappointing. Mom showed very little improvement; she was more alert and recognized who we were, but she was still confused and disoriented. She was not eating properly and she was uncooperative with the nurses. The doctor, as well as the nurses, informed us that if we wanted Mom to walk again and be self-sufficient, that she would have to be placed in a rehabilitation facility for a period of two or three months. The hospital was not equipped to render the type of physical therapy and rehabilitation she required. This was a total shock to us and we were not prepared for that kind of news. Once again, it was time to act and not react. Mom's health and welfare were most important; we had no choice but to give her the best medical care available. Mom was very resistant to the idea of being placed in a rehabilitation center; she cried and wanted to be taken home. We tried to convince her that if she wanted to heal and be able to walk again, that she had to go. I told her that it would be impossible for me to give her the extensive care she needed. Mom was very upset and resisted all our attempts to convince her it was the best thing for her. Since I had the power of attorney over her financial and health matters, I signed the necessary paperwork to transfer her from the hospital to the rehabilitation center. As much as I wanted Mom to come home, I had to do what was best for her. It was a heart-wrenching decision, but I had no other choice.

The next day, New Year's Eve, a private ambulance transported Mom, against her wishes, to the Queen's Boulevard Extended Care Facility. I followed the ambulance, and all the way there I was haunted with doubts regarding my decision. All I could do was hope and pray that Mom would soon come to realize that I acted in her best interests. All these years, Mom had been the strong one, the decision maker, the caretaker; now I had to step in and assume all the duties and responsibilities that she once commanded. It was a new role I had to accept, one I was totally unprepared for and reluctant to assume.

Mom was admitted and wheeled to a beautiful private room. The facility looked more like an expensive hotel than a hospital; everything was clean and it was well decorated. I was very pleased that it did not have an institutional appearance. Mom was not responsive to her surroundings; she still insisted vehemently on being taken home. I had to be firm and uncompromising with her and tell her she could not come home until she was walking and well again. She began crying and begging for me to obey her wishes. I told her she had no choice and that she had to accept the bitter facts and start adjusting to the situation. I had to resort to treating her like a child, telling her to be a good girl, and stop crying. At that point, I felt it best to let her settle into her new environment and get some rest. I told her I would be back in a little while; I kissed her on her forehead and told her I loved her.

Once again, when entering the house, there was that empty and cold feeling gripping at me. Just as I expected Mom to adjust to her new environment, I too had to adjust to mine. I felt lost and overwhelmed with all that was happening. It was all happening so fast, not leaving time to adapt; I had to resolutely deal with the problem and get on with the tasks at hand. There was no room for wallowing in self-pity or trying to avoid the inevitable. I had to muster up the strength needed and carry on. I not only had an obligation to take care of Mom, but I had the responsibilities of running my dental practice. I realized that both responsibilities would consume an inordinate amount of energy and time.

I called the rehab center to check on Mom and find out if she had settled down. The floor nurse informed me that she was quiet and resting; however, she was not eating. I asked if it would be all right to bring in some food from the outside for her to eat. She said it would be fine. I went to Dante's and ordered some pasta to go; maybe it would perk her up to have some nice Italian food for a change. I also brought from home some *Strega* to celebrate the New Year with Mom. I was hoping that it would bring back all her memories as a child and young woman growing up and facing new challenges and responsibilities every year. It certainly was going to be a new year, one filled with many new challenges and hurdles for both of us. I knew that at this point I had to be her pillar of strength, her guardian angel, her last refuge. Mom never backed down from her responsibilities or loyalty to her family, and out of love and respect for her; I was not going to back down from mine.

I had to force feed Mom her dinner; she fought me tooth and nail every step of the way. I told her if she didn't eat, she would not leave the rehab center, and that I would not take her home. It was very hard for me to treat Mom so sternly, but I had no choice. I reminded her of how stern and forceful she had to be with her sister when she broke her hip. If it weren't for her tough love, she would not have ever walked again. Mom seemed to comprehend what I was saying and responded with a reminiscent smile and sparkle in her eye. I was hoping that she would gain her self-confidence back and stop feeling sorry for herself. I had to give her some time to realize what she had to do to get back on her feet.

We toasted in the New Year early with a little sip of *Strega;* that brought a smile to Mom's face. I told her that this New Year was going to be only as good as she made it. I gave her the old army pep talk: fight, fight, fight! The day after tomorrow was a new beginning and she was to start her rehabilitation. She was tired, so I let her drift off to sleep. I decided to stay with her that evening; I slept in a chair in the hallway near her room. I, too, drifted off to sleep quickly.

The staff informed me the following day that Mom would be undergoing very intensive physical therapy beginning early in the morning and lasting until late in the afternoon. There would be short periods of rest in between treatment and at lunchtime. She would not be allowed to be in bed except at bedtime. They also told me that my visits would have to be limited to the evening hours after dinner. She would have to have all her meals in the dining room with the other patients. This was to be the routine seven days a week until she was able to walk on her own. I felt very confident with their methods and felt very secure in knowing that she was getting such concentrated and intensive treatment. I left that evening feeling elated that she was being taken care of so well. Now it was just a matter of time until Mom would be back on her feet and in her own home.

The next day I rearranged my work schedule at the office so I would be able to visit Mom after her dinner. I normally worked three evenings a week until 8 p.m. I changed my office hours so I would see my last patient at 4 p.m., allowing me sufficient time to go to the rehab center and spend a few hours with Mom before she went to sleep. I knew this new routine would be very exhausting and consume my whole day. I ate my dinners late at night after Mom went to sleep. In a way, the long hours kept me occupied and alleviated my loneliness and the empty feelings I felt about being in Mom's house alone. The only time I spent in the house was to sleep.

I visited Mom that first day of her therapy after she had dinner. I was surprised to see her sitting up in a chair watching television in the recreation room at the end of the hall. She appeared somewhat tired, but more alert and responsive than I had seen in the past week. She was excited to see me and gave me a big hug and kiss. She filled me in on the events of the day, sounding like a little girl relating everything she did on her first day of the new school year. I was relieved to see her in such good spirits.

Mom appeared to be making progress every day, even though she still complained of pain in her hip. I tried to reassure her that it was all part of the healing process and the pain would diminish gradually over the next few weeks. The major portion of the pain came from the physical stress of the therapy, and the remainder was the remnants of the surgery. The staff informed me that Mom would continue to experience twinges of pain long after leaving the rehab center and that it was nothing to be overly concerned with as long as the pain did not keep her from being mobile. Mild analgesics would make her comfortable and allow her to ambulate and be active rather than be sedentary. I began to realize that Mom's rehabilitation was going to be a long drawn out affair and far more extensive once she left the rehab center. I had to start planning a course of action and prepare for an arduous and grueling routine of homecare.

Needless to say, my days were long and draining, but I'm sure Mom's days were more strenuous and exhausting. She displayed a lot of strong will and determination coupled with an unusual amount of energy for a ninety-year-old woman. She realized that she had to lay aside her frailty and pain, and concentrate on regaining her strength and independence. Every day brought new and improved results, both mentally and physically. I had arranged for Mom to have regularly scheduled appointments a few times a week at the beauty parlor in the rehab center. This no doubt aided in lifting her spirits and making her feel spryer. Mom was always concerned with her appearance and I wanted to make sure she maintained her elegant and stylish facade.

As the weeks dragged on, Mom was chomping at the bit to come home. I was also anxious to have her home, but I had to heed to the judgment and recommendations of the rehab staff. When they felt she was ready to be released, then she would come home, and not a day sooner. Even though Mom had made great strides in her recovery and therapy, she was still dependent on a walker and the assistance of an aide to be able to walk around. Once she arrived at the stage where she could walk alone and unassisted with only a cane, she would be ready to be released. Their goal for Mom was total and independent mobility. They were the experts and I had no choice but to listen to their advice and guidance if I wanted the best for her. Mom was a little disappointed in knowing that she still had quite a hurdle to overcome. I convinced her that once she was able to walk with a cane, she would be back in her own home, and able to be somewhat independent and mobile.

The next few weeks seemed like an eternity. Mom was still dependent on the walker and very fearful of shedding it in anticipation of falling. I had to respect her fears, but by the same token, I had to convey the point to her that she would never be independent unless she gained the confidence of walking with a cane as her only means of support. It was a Herculean task to overcome her fear, but a necessary one. Once again, I had to hope and pray that Mom would rise to the occasion and realize what she had to do. Now it was a matter of will, not physical ability. The nurses reassured her and me that she was physically capable of walking with a cane and that it was only a matter of fear that was holding her back from independence.

Mom quickly responded to all our wishes and started to overcome her fear. She started taking tiny steps with the cane while being supported under her arm by an aide. She was still timid and reluctant to be left alone without the help of the aide, but at least she was making progress. The next few days proved to be inspiring and hopeful. Mom was ambulating up and down the halls with only minimal support from the aide. The head therapist informed me that I should now make plans to take Mom home the following week. After six long weeks of agonizing and intensive treatment, Mom's dream of coming home was a reality. Her hard work and determination had paid off, and she was returning to her palace.

Chapter 11

The Homecoming, Continued Care, Total Commitment

Preparing for Mom's homecoming required an inordinate amount of planning and organization. Because Mom was not able to go upstairs to her bedroom to sleep, I had to rearrange the downstairs living room and set it up as her living quarters. I brought a bed downstairs from the guest room and set it up close to the stairway so I would be able to hear her if she needed me during the night. I also moved her clothes and dresser into the den and the downstairs closets. Having everything on the first floor would make it easy for Mom to get around and not worry about climbing stairs. The first floor also had a full bathroom, making it very convenient for her to take care of her personal hygiene needs. I also moved tables and lamps around to make it easier to walk around without having to navigate through a lot of clutter and cumbersome furniture. I also set up a wireless listening device similar to those used by parents to monitor a baby's cries during the night.

Since I had not eaten at home for the past six weeks, the refrigerator was empty. I had to stock the refrigerator with the basic staples. Then the panic set in; how were we to eat? I did not know how to cook and I knew Mom would not be able to cook for a long time; she would not be able to stand for that long a period to prepare meals. Fortunately, the neighborhood we lived in had a vast amount of restaurants and delicatessens right around the corner from us. It would be easy for me to bring in a wide variety of meals for lunch and dinner. I also filled the cupboards with snacks and munchies.

The rehab center informed me that Mom was entitled to three weeks of homecare provided by social services. I arranged for an aide to take care of Mom from 9 a.m. until 3 p.m. The aide would bathe and dress Mom and attend to her as needed. Once again, I had to rearrange my office hours so I could be home when the aide left at the end of her shift. The only haunting concern I had was what was going to happen when the three weeks were up and I was left alone with Mom. I could not leave her alone during the day for fear she might not be able to take care of herself safely and properly. That bridge would have to be crossed later; the main thing was that Mom was coming home and we would have some help for a few weeks.

The day I was to pick up Mom happened to fall on Valentine's Day. I bought her a dozen roses and placed them on the dining room table. I also purchased for her a CD of her favorite Italian songs sung by Luciano Pavarotti to play in the car on the drive back home; I thought that would make her happy. When I arrived in front of the rehab center early that morning, Mom was outside with one of her aides standing with only the support of her cane. When she saw me get out of the car, her face lit up. She hugged and kissed me. We both thanked the aide and said good-bye. I placed her suitcase in the trunk, escorted her into the passenger's seat, and placed her seat belt on. She looked at me with tears in her eyes and motioned for us to go. When I turned on the car stereo, tears flowed down her face; tears of joy, for she knew she was going back to her world, her home, and her palace.

When we pulled into the driveway alongside the house, she uttered a sigh of relief and just said, "My palace." I brought her into the house through the front entrance. When she entered and saw the flowers and her familiar surroundings, she turned and hugged and kissed me, and thanked me for standing by her and making this day possible. Needless to say, it was a very emotional and unforgettable moment for both of us. She was now home, safe and secure in her own environment after six long and grueling weeks. She walked very slowly and wide-eyed through all the rooms, noting all her treasured possessions. Mom seemed to accept the rearrangements I made so that she would be able to remain on one floor. Overall, she was happy and content with being back in her own home.

Mom was a little tired from all the excitement connected with her leaving the rehab center and coming home. I sat her in the recliner in the den and placed a light blanket on her. She dozed off quickly, allowing me a little time to unpack her clothes and review the written instructions from the nurses regarding her medications. I had to make sure I gave her all her medication at the proper intervals. I arranged to take off from work for a few days so I myself could adjust to what had to be done for Mom. I wanted to be home when the aide came the next day, so I could make sure she was taken care of properly. I had a lot to learn about taking care of an elderly woman; I knew it would not be easy, but somehow I felt driven to overcome my trepidation and concentrate on what had to be done. I had no choice; I would not put Mom in a nursing home and cast her aside. She was still a vibrant and spry woman; all she needed was some time to regain her strength and independence.

Mom woke up after a brief nap; she appeared somewhat rejuvenated and alert. She did, however, express some discomfort with her hip. I gave her some over-the-counter pain reliever to ease her pain. It was getting late in the afternoon and I had to plan some kind of a meal for both of us. Mom expressed a desire for some good old-fashioned pizza, something she had not had in a long time. I knew it was not the best thing to have for dinner, but I felt that she was entitled to a special treat if that was her choice. I turned on the television and left her sitting in the recliner while I went around the corner to the local pizzeria. When I returned home, I found Mom sitting at the kitchen table waiting anxiously for her food. I opened up a bottle of wine and we had a party!

Mom was thrilled to have eaten in her own kitchen again; we toasted with a glass of *Strega* to celebrate her return. I escorted her to her recliner in the den and had her watch television while I cleaned up in the kitchen. When I returned, she was fast asleep. It was a long and emotional-day for her, and she was exhausted. I woke her up after a few minutes and told her it would be better for her if she slept in her bed. She was a little reluctant to go to bed; it was strange for her to be sleeping in the living room all alone. I reassured her that even though I would be sleeping upstairs, I would be close by and be able to hear her if she needed me. She changed into her nightgown and I tucked her in bed and kissed her good night. She thanked me for everything and told me I was the whole world to her. I felt like she was a child and I was now the parent. It was a strange yet satisfying feeling, knowing that I was responsible for her care and wellbeing.

I left a table lamp on in the dining room so she was not left alone in total darkness. I, too, was exhausted from the day's events and went upstairs to my room. I dozed off quickly into a deep sleep only to be wakened by Mom's calling out to me. I ran downstairs, found her crying, and very upset. She had awoken in pain and was confused and frightened by her unfamiliar surroundings. I gave her some over-the-counter pain medication and tried to alleviate her fear. She wanted to go upstairs to her own bedroom. I told her that it was impossible because she was unable to climb that many stairs and that she could fall again causing her to be put back into the hospital. I felt I had to scare her into submission; that was the only way I could reason with her. It was a reality that she had to deal with and accept. After a short bout of wits, she reluctantly gave in to my demands. I did not want to leave her downstairs alone while she was still upset and in pain, so I told her I would get a pillow and blanket and sleep on the floor next to her. That seemed to calm her and make her feel more secure. Needless to say, I spent a very uncomfortable night on the floor listening for any sounds of pain or discomfort.

Mom was still sleeping soundly when I woke up. I went upstairs to get dressed and then suddenly realized that I had to feed Mom some kind of breakfast; another dilemma! I had stocked the refrigerator with eggs, bread, and coffee, but I did not know how to cook, and I certainly didn't expect Mom to make breakfast for herself. I quickly ran to the bagel shop around the corner and brought home a few bagels and cream cheese and two cups of coffee. I figured that would hold her until the aide came and made her something more substantial. Mom woke up and was a little groggy, but she was delighted to see the bagels and coffee on the kitchen table; it was a treat for her. I checked her blood sugar level as instructed by the nurses and made sure she took all her morning medication before eating. Even though it was not the most nutritious meal I could serve her, Mom savored and relished every mouthful. We sat around the table after breakfast and made small talk while we waited for the homecare aide to arrive. I was a little apprehensive and anxious to see who would be taking care of Mom. Since I would be at work most of the day, I wanted to make sure that she was in reliable and caring hands.

The front door bell rang promptly at nine; I opened the door, greeted the aide, and ushered her in from the cold. She was a tall and neatly-dressed young woman from South Africa named Shurina; she was very shy and soft spoken. I brought her into the kitchen to meet Mom. She addressed her as "mum" and softly held her hand in a lovingly and concerned manner. Mom responded to her very warmly with a big smile, one of approval. Shurina told Mom she was going to take her to the bathroom to wash and dress her. She helped Mom up ever-so-gently and securely held her arm as they left the kitchen. I was very impressed with Shurina as to how she attended to Mom in such a caring and gentle way. I took the free time while they were in the bathroom to go upstairs and get some of my personal chores done. It was a very comforting feeling to know someone else was there to help me with Mom; especially with her personal hygiene needs.

When I returned downstairs after a short while, I found Mom in her recliner with Shurina kneeling beside her, applying moisturizer on Mom's arms and legs. Mom was dressed in a beautiful housecoat and her hair was nicely coiffed. She looked so relaxed and tranquil and totally at ease with Shurina. They were engaged in a light conversation as Shurina massaged Mom while they both watched television. What a wonderful spectacle it was to see Mom and Shurina interact so easily. I was more than pleased for both Mom and me.

Since I knew Mom was in safe hands, I decided to go to my office for an hour just to check on things. When I returned home, I found Mom and Shurina in the kitchen having lunch, talking, and laughing. Mom was entertaining Shurina with one of her many famous stories of her past as a young woman. Mom was perky and vibrant as she spoke; it was a delight to see her so animated and effervescent. They seemed like two schoolchildren giggling over the trivial events in their lives. I joined them and could not help but notice how well Mom interacted with Shurina. The afternoon flew by quickly and it was time for Shurina to leave. She took Mom back into the den for a little nap before dinner. We were sorry to see her leave; it felt like a good friend and companion was leaving after a big party. We both anxiously anticipated her return the next day.

After Mom awoke from her nap, we talked a while about the day and how pleased we both were with Shurina. She was a true blessing. Now that we were left alone again, we had to plan dinner—yes, take-out again! Mom expressed a desire for some Chinese food. We were lucky to have so many diverse and ethnic restaurants available in the neighborhood. It was another dinner party with the two of us, complete with fortune cookies. After dinner, we both retired to the den to watch television, a common routine we were settling into. Mom appeared very relaxed and had a look of contentment on her face. I could tell she was very happy with the way the day turned out. I gave Mom her evening medications and she got herself ready for bed. I tucked her in and assured her that tomorrow would even be a better day. She smiled and kissed me good night. I sat in the chair next to her bed and waited for her to doze off before I went back to the den. She quickly fell into a deep and restful sleep, giving me a little more peace of mind. I relaxed for an hour or so before retiring for the night.

I awoke early the next morning and quietly came downstairs; Mom was still sleeping. I decided to let her get her rest until Shurina arrived. Mom was scheduled to have a home visit by the physical therapist that morning. She would receive therapy three times a week for two weeks and a visiting registered nurse would also come twice a week. I was very pleased with the way Mom was being monitored by all the healthcare professionals. Shurina had informed me the day before that she would make breakfast for Mom when she arrived. That was a big help for me, since I didn't have to leave Mom alone to run out in the early wintry morning and catch a chill. Shurina arrived right on schedule and started breakfast immediately. She got Mom up and escorted her to the kitchen. She had prepared a very nice and nutritious breakfast not only for Mom but for me as well. I was very surprised and deeply grateful.

The therapist arrived shortly after Shurina had gotten Mom all cleaned up and dressed. He gave her quite a workout; I don't think Mom was expecting such an intensive session. She was exhausted from all the leg lifts and walking. He instructed me to make her do all the exercises he showed her every day. The exercises were intended to stretch and strengthen her muscles. He did not want her to just sit around the house all day and develop atrophy of her muscles. Shurina was instructed to keep her both physically and mentally active during the hours she was there. Mom was a little reticent with the whole idea of being monitored so closely, but ultimately she understood it was for her own good.

The visiting nurse arrived in the early afternoon and she too was very thorough. She took Mom's blood pressure, temperature, respiration rate, weight, and blood sugar level. She conversed quite extensively with Mom to determine her mental acuity and alertness. She was very surprised to see how sharp and alert Mom was for a ninety-year-old woman. She instructed us that an important part of her home rehabilitation and healing was mental stimulation by conversation and playing certain games, especially card games. She also told us that while a nap in the afternoon was therapeutic and rejuvenating, it should be no longer than one-half of an hour. A longer nap would only make her lethargic and sluggish. In addition, she wanted Mom to be fully dressed each and every day; also a psychological component of her therapy.

After having physical therapy and the visit by the nurse, Mom was both physically and mentally exhausted. Shurina gave her a gentle moisturizing massage and let her nap for a while. While Mom slept, Shurina and I reviewed the instructions given to us by the therapist and nurse, just to make sure we both understood every detail that was involved. We wrote down everything that was told to us and kept the sheet handy so we would both have easy access to it. It became very apparent to me how involved and meticulous we had to be in our handling of Mom. There was a lot more to homecare than meets the eye. It was a full-time job, an obligation with constant vigilance and commitment to duty. It was a twenty-four-hour, seven-day-a-week commitment that I gladly accepted out of love and respect for Mom. I was grateful that I had Shurina during the week to help share the responsibility; it was the weekends where I would be alone with Mom that I was a little reluctant to take care of all her needs by myself.

Mom awoke from her nap shortly before Shurina was to leave for the day. Once again, we were both very grateful and appreciative for all the help and caring she gave to us. After Shurina left, we were once again faced with the recurring dilemma of what to eat for dinner. By now, we both realized that a constant diet of take-out food was not the most healthy way to eat, nor was it the most economical. It was time for us to put our heads together and come up with a suitable and appropriate alternative. We both knew it was too difficult a task for Mom to prepare and serve dinner by herself. Mom, being the definitive and adept teacher that she was her whole life, came up with the solution. She was going to teach me how to cook. I looked at her in utter amazement and shock! I, who had never even boiled water during my entire life, was going to learn how to cook. Mom reassured me that with her teaching skills and my ability to pay attention to detail, it would be easy and fun. I succumbed to her suggestion, realizing something had to be done about our eating situation, and that it would be mentally stimulating for Mom once again to take on the role of the teacher. Killing two birds with one stone!

Mom made a list of fresh ingredients for me to purchase from the vegetable store around the corner. Our first homemade meal cooked by me was going to be a simple pasta dish with marinara sauce. Mom was excited and exuberant, and I was reticent and nervous. Now I had to sink or swim; dive in headfirst and let the tide take me on a new journey down uncharted waters. Nothing ventured, nothing gained! When I returned from the store, Mom sat me down and outlined what I was to accomplish. It was a real teaching lesson, replete with the chemistry of cooking and the terminology of the preparatory steps. Since I had spent a major portion of my life in higher education and science, I was not averse to learning. I looked upon cooking as just another chemistry project—meticulous attention to detail and the appropriate quantity of ingredients equals a final result; in the case of cooking, it would hopefully be a gustatory delight.

My first meal prepared under the watchful and scrutinizing eye of my mother turned out to my amazement to be quite delicious. Mom was very pleased with my performance and I was very proud of my accomplishment. We celebrated my endeavor with a glass of *Strega!* What I thought would be a Herculean task turned out to be a simple scientific experiment. I was ready and eager to learn more and move on to more intricate and elaborate meals. Mom held the reins and tried to curb my zealous urges, stating that there were still many more basics I had to learn. She didn't try to thwart my enthusiasm, only control the pace of my progression. Little did I know that I was embarking on a long and fruitful venture that would provide me with countless hours of enjoyment and my family with numerous pleasing and delicious meals.

Every afternoon, when I came home from work and Shurina had left for the day, Mom and I would sit down for a new cooking lesson. Each meal became more and more intricate and elaborate, requiring more complicated preparation, finer ingredients, and much more attention to detail. Mom was a great teacher, and luckily, I was a good student and a fast learner. Mom's cooking lessons proved to be the best therapy for her. She became excited and animated with each and every lesson. She smiled, laughed, and was full of life. It was very rewarding for me to see Mom so happy and alive.

Mom progressed very well with her physical therapy and we were all pleased with the results. She was no longer dependent on her cane for support and she walked without a limp. She still required help dressing and bathing, but overall, she was becoming self-sufficient. As the weeks flew by, spring was around the corner and the time when Shurina would leave was close at hand. Mom and I were both dreading that day. Shurina had become such a close and warm friend and companion for Mom. She helped fill Mom's day while I was at work and it was a great comfort for me to know that Mom was not alone and idle. I could see that as the day for her to leave was drawing nearer, she too was becoming sad and upset. She had developed a genuine love and respect for Mom. I approached Shurina and asked her if she would consider a full-time position as companion and aide to Mom. I offered her a substantial increase over the salary she was making at the agency for which she worked. She gleefully accepted my offer and ran to Mom's arms, crying for joy. She and Mom embraced and I could see the look of peace and contentment in Mom's face. She was overjoyed at knowing that Shurina would be with her every day during the week. I was relieved and thankful that Mom was happy and was in loving and kind hands.

My culinary skills were improving rapidly as the months went by. I became more confident and self-assured in my ability to prepare a vast array of meals. I decided one day to invite Diana from next door to join us for dinner. She gladly accepted and was incredibly surprised to learn that I prepared the meal myself. She, being a wonderful cook herself, was shocked and impressed with how delicious the meal was. She helped foster my confidence and gave me supportive encouragement and accolades. Having Diana over for dinner was now to become a routine; it was another source of entertainment and companionship for Mom. It became a party for Mom, and they both enjoyed reminiscing about the old days. Diana always loved and respected Mom, and she enjoyed being part of the family. I was glad to include Diana in our family meals. I was proud to be able to cook for and entertain her. She was a dear and close long-time friend.

Now that the weather was warm and the snow was gone, I was able to take Mom out of the house and take her out for dinner to break-up the monotony of being cooped up in the house all day. I would stroll with Mom around the corner and for a few blocks to the Sly Fox for an early dinner. It was good exercise for her to walk and she enjoyed getting out for a change of pace. Joe, the owner, loved seeing Mom and always made a fuss over her. Everyone there, from Joe's partner Eddie, the managers Doug and Deedee, the bartenders Joey, Danny, Carle, and John, to the waitresses Diane, Chris, and Norma, were enthralled with her stories. They all treated Mom with the utmost respect and admiration. Mom felt like a queen every time we went there. She loved to sit in the pub area because there was always a lot of activity going on. Many friends of mine would also stop by, say hello to Mom, patiently and respectfully sit, and listen to her many stories of her past. Mom loved the attention and I got a kick out of seeing the wide-eyed expression on her face as she recanted her youth and adventures. On the walk home, Mom would always tell me what a wonderful time she had. She was always appreciative of all the small and simple things I did for her. She was very easy to please.

Our weekends were spent mostly alone, occasionally broken up by a Sunday dinner at Tony and Judy's. I did manage to take Mom on some short trips to visit family in Connecticut and Vermont. Mom was not fond of long drives nor did she want to be away from her home for any more than a few days. She was a creature of habit and relished her home surroundings. Every time we returned home from a trip or even from dining out, Mom always made the comment when entering her house, "Home, sweet home, be it ever so humble." I tried as best as I could to upkeep and maintain her home the way she preferred it. Over the years, certain things had become dated and worn out. I decided to treat Mom to a total overhaul and renovation of her house. Mom really did not want to change anything but I convinced her that certain improvements would add greatly to her comfort and security.

Once I started the renovations, one thing led to another. New windows required a new and updated alarm and security system. New carpeting led to reupholstering the furniture and new window treatments. I replaced the antiquated heating system with a new gas burner. A new kitchen sink led to counters and appliances. Painting and wallpaper were the final additions inside. The outside entailed new landscaping with underground sprinkler system, a new porch with railing, pointing of all outside bricks, and the addition of a large deck off the den with new outdoor furniture and barbeque. When it was all done, Mom was very pleased with the changes. She loved her new palace. Mom would spend countless hours sitting outside on the front porch with either me or Shurina, watching all the neighbors passing by and the children playing.

I spent a lot of time at home with Mom, making sure she was comfortable and secure. I was fortunate that I was able to be away from my office as much as I was. I had two associate doctors and an incredibly efficient staff running my office. The real strength and backbone of my office consisted of my competent, proficient, well-organized, and professional girls whom have been in my employ for many years. Their dedication and loyalty to me has led to the success of my practice. Sharon, Sharlene, Milagros, Mary, and Maria are like family to me. They have been an integral part of my professional as well as my personal life. They also loved Mom and showed her an inordinate amount of respect. Mom was very fond of all "My Girls."

Mom was always very conscious of her appearance; she loved being coiffed. Every other week or so I would bring her to the beauty parlor in the neighborhood to have her hair colored and nails manicured. She relished the pampering and always felt like a queen when she was finished. I would take her out that evening for a special dinner to either Dante's or the Sly Fox. She would get all dressed up as if she were going to a ball. She loved all the attention and accolades people gave her when they saw her. Mom was always appreciative and happy on our little special nights out. I felt it was another way to add diversity and stimulation to her life. For me, it was rewarding to know that I could help preserve her vitality and mental wellbeing. I loved seeing her happy and content, and free of worry.

Summer was drawing to an end and I wanted to make sure the fall and winter would not be boring for Mom by being shut in the house all the time. Since Mom had always loved the opera, I thought it would be entertaining for her to attend a few performances. I wanted to do for her as she had often told me she did for her parents when she was a young woman. I arranged for season tickets to the Metropolitan Opera at Lincoln Center. I presented them to her on her on her ninety-first birthday. When she opened the envelope containing the tickets, she froze momentarily, then clasped her hands together as if in prayer, and tears cascaded down her cheeks. She had never thought that she would ever go to the opera again in her life. The joy and pleasure that I felt at that moment was inexplicable. How such a small thing could bring such joy to a person was unbelievable—to Mom it was as if I had given her a treasure chest full of gold and diamonds.

For the next several weeks prior to the first operatic performance, Mom was planning what she was going to wear. She had Shurina help her upstairs to her closets where she had stored all her formal gowns in search of the perfect outfit for opening night. She had Shurina lay everything out from gown to opera length gloves on the bed for her inspection. Even Diana came over to help put together an ensemble for Mom. It was as if Mom were a teenager getting ready to go to her senior prom. I, too, made sure I was dressed properly by going out and purchasing a new tuxedo for the occasion. It was to be a gala affair. Our seats were box seats in dress circle; nothing but the best for a woman who always gave her best to everyone.

That magical day arrived, and when I came downstairs after getting dressed, Mom was standing in the living room all decked out in her best attire. She was Cinderella waiting to go to the ball. Diana was there and she took pictures of us prior to our departure for opening night at the Met. I had arranged for a limousine to take us into the city for a quick dinner and then to Lincoln Center. I escorted Mom into the limo and off we went on a fairytale adventure. Mom, with a frozen smile and twinkling eyes, clasped my hand in silence all the way into the city. It almost seemed that if she would let go of my hand, the fairytale would end. After dinner, our limo left us off at Lincoln Center, with instructions to pick us up after the performance. We slowly walked across the brilliantly illuminated courtyard, past the magnificent flowing fountains, and entered the opera house. Mom's eyes gazed at all the extravagant and spectacular surroundings like a child seeing the circus for the first time.

When the curtain opened and the orchestra began playing, Mom's attention never left the stage. She quietly sang along with the ensemble to all the arias. I just kept looking at her face and pondered about how she must have felt with her parents so many years ago. Bringing enjoyment to someone you love is internally rewarding and gratifying; there is so much truth in the saying that there is more joy in giving than in receiving. Now I know why my mother had so much self-satisfaction and inner peace during her whole life. I, too, have now experienced that wonderful and peaceful feeling and the internal reward of serenity and contentment that caring and giving to others bestows upon you.

Chapter 12

She Fell from Heaven, Shared Joy, A New Beginning

Mom was well on her way to a full recovery from her fall. Time has a way of healing all wounds, both physical and emotional. The days and weeks were flying by and the months rapidly turning into years. I basically maintained a mundane routine of working and taking care of Mom. It was a simple but satisfying existence, one of choice and commitment. Things do change from time to time, and adjustments had to be made. Shurina became pregnant and it was necessary for her to terminate her employment with us. She arranged for her niece, Linda, who was here on a student visa, to fill in for her and attend school at night. We were very sad to lose Shurina; she was like part of the family. She loved and respected Mom so much that she named her baby daughter Louise. That made Mom so proud and happy.

I continued cooking under the limited tutelage of Mom, but I had progressed to the point where I was experimenting on my own with new recipes. Cooking was a great way to fill my time; it became a hobby and a pastime. The majority of my cooking was still the old-world basic Italian meals I grew up eating. I now had the confidence to share my culinary skills with many friends and family members. Whenever Italians cook, even if it is for two people, there is always plenty left over to share with other people. Joe, from the Sly Fox, loved Italian food and he always expressed a desire to taste some of my dishes. One evening, after Mom and I had finished dinner, Mom had suggested that I bring a plate of the leftover pasta to Joe. I carefully wrapped up the pasta in a container and brought it over to him. Bringing food to a restaurant was out of the ordinary to say the least. When I presented the dish to Joe, he devoured the pasta as if he had not seen or eaten food in days. He was absolutely thrilled and delighted with my sauce and I was elated with his accolades and praises. It became routine two or three times a week for me to bring leftovers to the Sly Fox. A few times, when Joe was not there, some of the waitresses and bartenders would share the dish. After a few weeks, whenever I walked in with a dish of food, a hungry and begging crowd surrounded me. They all loved my food, and I loved the attention.

Wednesday at the restaurant was pasta night, and it was suggested that I make the sauce for the customers. It was a very tempting and flattering proposal, but I didn't want to be responsible for cooking in such volume on a routine basis. I was also approached by several employees and customers to sell them containers of my different sauces. I was proud of my sauces, and accepted the offer. What started out as a lark turned into a full-time proposition. I began making and freezing large containers of all kinds of Italian sauces. Every night I would carry over bags full of the sauce people had ordered. It became fun and exciting, a new popularity I had never anticipated. Mom really enjoyed my endeavor too. She loved to watch me cook and relished the thought that all her efforts in teaching me how to cook turned out to be so fulfilling for me.

Mom was very self-sufficient by now and was comfortable with putting herself to bed at night without me there. She felt that since she retired early every night, there was no reason for me always to be at home in the early evening. She wanted me to have some time with my friends and relax. I was reluctant to leave her alone at first, but she reassured me she would be fine. I generally went out around 7 p.m. and came home around 9 p.m. She had the phone number where I was and she wore a medical alert device around her neck in case of an emergency. After dinner on a few nights a week, I cleaned up the dishes and made sure Mom was securely sitting in the den watching television before I went out. I enjoyed getting out, especially the nights when there was music and dancing. I never stayed out late during the week because I had to be up early in the morning to let Linda in and then get myself ready for work.

One particular evening, while I was at the Sly Fox sitting by myself listening to the music and observing the crowd of people, I noticed an individual character roaming around the bar and inching his way in close to several girls as they conversed with each other. His behavior was quite inappropriate and crude. The girls he made contact with were oblivious to the movement of his hands and made no protest. I observed him as he sauntered around the rectangular shaped bar making several stops along the way, as if he were on a tour. He continued his lurking promenade in my direction and I noticed that he set his sights on two girls sitting about ten feet to my left. When he started his move in their direction, I instinctively got up from my stool, boldly went over to one of the girls, and put my arm around her waist as if to give the appearance that we were together, hoping this character would bypass her. The young woman naturally and unsurprisingly questioned my actions. I explained to her what my intentions were and what was happening as I directed her attention to the individual as he continued his prowling. I thought for a moment that my chivalrous and gallant behavior might have sparked some indignation from her, but instead she very politely and graciously thanked me. We cordially exchanged introductions, and as we conversed, I became mesmerized by her overall beauty and elegance. Her warm and enchanting smile was captivating and her sparkling golden hazel eyes were entrancing. She was a true vision of loveliness and beauty.

The more we spoke, the more we learned about each other. I learned that her unusual name, Hennie, came from her father, who was a professional boxer; Hennie was his ring name. She was once a professional high-fashion model in New York City, working for many well-known fashion houses, and had even appeared on the outside advertisements on city buses. I wasn't surprised that she was a model because she looked absolutely stunning and radiant. It took me awhile, but I mustered up enough nerve to ask her to dance, and she accepted. When I saw her dance and glide on the dance floor I became once again enthralled with her beauty, but this time it was her tall and shapely figure and how she flowed with the music. She was beautiful from head to toe. I couldn't take my eyes off her! We danced and talked for several hours that evening and the time seemed to fly by. It was getting very late and I had to leave to get back to Mom; I wasn't accustomed to staying out so late and leaving Mom for any great length of time. I explained my situation to Hennie and she understood fully. I wasn't able to acquire her phone number, but I gave her my business card along with my home phone number and told her that I would really like to see her again if she was so inclined.

When I got home, Mom was sleeping soundly as usual. I sat down in the den and was reflecting on the magical evening I had just spent with Hennie. She certainly was a lovely girl and I would have loved to see her again, but, in my heart of hearts, I knew that given my commitments to work and caring for Mom, it would be nearly impossible to have a relationship with anyone at this time. I reconciled myself to the fact that I had to stay focused on my obligations, and put my feelings on the back burner. That evening I spent dancing and talking to Hennie was a special gift from God; it was as if she fell from heaven to give me a reprieve from my mundane and unexciting existence. I kept thinking about her sparkling eyes and how they lit up every time she smiled. Her charm and beauty filled my thoughts as I dozed off to sleep.

My mind was preoccupied with thoughts of Hennie the whole next day. As much as I was enamored with her, I kept pondering over the fact that this was not the right time in my life to enter into a relationship with a young woman. My responsibilities to my practice and my obligations to my mother were just about all I could handle at this time. I felt a little disheartened about the fact that there was no room in my life for anything other than my work as doctor and caregiver to my mother. My divorce three years earlier had placed my desire for emotional entanglement on hold and I was very reluctant to get involved ever again. Up until now, I had not felt the absence of my own need for happiness and romance. I never really felt that my situation was a sacrifice; I always considered it my obligation and duty as a son. I was never bitter or complained; I felt proud of myself for what I was doing and I did it with love and enthusiasm. We all strive in one way or another to achieve a fulfilling and happy life, yet there is no perfect existence. We all have to deal with life's adversities and certain hardships, and we still survive. My life, while complete and rewarding in so many ways, was empty in others. The only panacea for true happiness is to do the best with what you have and try to enjoy the beautiful moments and experiences that come from life as it exists.

For the next several weeks, life as I knew it was continuing at the same pace. Mom was doing well and I was plugging along as usual. I continued to make my Italian sauces and bring selected dishes to the Sly Fox for people to savor. One night when I was there, Eddie informed me that Hennie had come in with her friend Linda the night before and that I had missed her by not being there. I was a little disappointed that I didn't get a chance to see her again. Since I did not have her phone number, I had no way of reaching her and she had not called me. I found out from Eddie that she was going through a rather difficult divorce and she probably was just as reluctant to date as I was. She had three teenage children and it was a very difficult time for her. I fully understood her situation and felt sorry for her. I just wished I had the opportunity to see her again and spend some time dancing and chatting and just having a pleasant evening together. Since she was not dating, just meeting at the Sly Fox and spending a few hours together would be all I could hope for at this time. I went home that evening rather upset that I had missed seeing Hennie.

As fate would have it, I did get to see Hennie again one night when the DJ was at the Fox. I had brought in one of my Italian specialties as usual that night and offered Hennie some to taste. It was a good excuse to go over to her and strike up a conversation. She appeared happy to see me and she enjoyed sampling my food. We made small talk and once again danced when the music started. She seemed more relaxed and comfortable with me than the first time I met her. She was as radiant and beautiful as the first time I laid eyes on her. When we danced to the slow tunes, I felt electricity when holding her. She was so warm and soft to hold and the aroma of her perfume was like an opiate; it mesmerized me. We spent the evening together talking and dancing. When the evening ended, we planned to meet again the following weekend. It really wasn't a set date, but we both understood it was a chance to see each other again.

Hennie and I met each other at the Fox on a regular basis, never really dating, but it was mutually understood that we were together for the evening. At the end of the evening, I would walk home and she would leave with her friend Linda. This type of rendezvous continued for several weeks until Eddie suggested that he, Linda, Hennie, and I go out for dinner one evening together. I had lost a golf bet with Eddie and I owed him a dinner; it turned out to be a great way for me to go out with Hennie on a real date. I asked her if she was comfortable with the idea of a dinner date and she consented, but with one condition: that I pick her up at her parents' home, where she was living. I agreed and the date was set!

It had been quite a few years since I had actually gone out on a date and I was a little nervous about starting again. I felt like I was going to my first school dance. That evening when I was to pick up Hennie, I fed Mom an early dinner and explained to her that I was having dinner with a friend. Mom was very self-sufficient now so it was all right for me to leave her alone in the evening for a few hours as long as I didn't make it a late night. Mom was fine with the idea of me going out with a friend, but I don't think she knew it was a female and that it was a date. When I got dressed and was ready to leave, Mom gave me one of those "mother looks" that said have a good time and be careful; I think she surmised that I had a date by the way I was dressed and how nervous I acted. I was reluctant to tell Mom I had met someone only because I felt she might not understand how I needed something more in my life at this time. To her, my life seemed complicated enough with work and taking care of her. She was right in a sense, but she was probably not taking into consideration my emotional needs. I myself had mixed emotions about getting involved with a young woman again, but I felt a little female companionship would be healthy and gratifying.

When I arrived at Hennie's parents' home that evening, I had a queasy feeling in my stomach as I approached the front door. Here I was, fifty-five years old and picking up a girl at her parents' home for our first date. My adrenalin was pumping and my heart was fluttering. Her mother answered the door and invited me in. As we exchanged introductions, I was very surprised to see how young both her parents looked. Hennie's mother could have passed for my older sister and her father was tall, slim, and well built. Now I knew where Hennie got her good looks. They were both very warm and cordial to me as I waited for Hennie. When Hennie came into the living room, I was once again taken back by her beauty and stature. She was beautifully dressed and looked like she had just stepped out of *Vogue* magazine. She sure had a flare for style and knew how to wear clothing well.

We politely made our exit and as we entered my car, we both breathed a sigh of relief. It was a tense situation for both of us, since we felt like children all over again. We soon began to relax and get comfortable with each other on the way to the restaurant. We met Eddie and Linda at the restaurant and proceeded to have an enjoyable and relaxing time. After dinner, we all went back to the Fox for after dinner drinks and to dance and listen to music. For me, it was a magical evening, everything was perfect. I took Hennie home rather early, once again explaining my situation about not wanting to stay out late and leaving Mom alone for too long a period. She was very understanding and accommodating. We were both very comfortable with each other and happy our first date went so well. I think for the both of us, getting the first official date over with was a big hurdle to overcome. It was hard for me to enter the dating scene after so many years, and I know Hennie felt the same way. Divorce leaves certain scars that seem to linger too long.

Hennie and I had frequent dinner dates and our relationship became more and more comfortable for both of us. We got along very well together and it seemed we were made for each other. We shared many common interests and, of course, we both loved dancing. At the Fox, we were always on the dance floor and at times, it was just the two of us dancing, oblivious to the fact that we were the only ones dancing. When I held Hennie in my arms, all sense of time seemed to evaporate and all I thought about and felt was her warmth and tenderness. She had an alluring effect on me that was magical and mystifying. After our dates, when I would be home in bed, the warm and delicate lingering aroma of her perfume anesthetized me to sleep as I thought of her.

My birthday was just around the corner and Mom had wanted to take me out for dinner to celebrate. She asked me if I wanted to have Hennie join us for dinner. Since Mom had not met her yet, I thought it would be a perfect opportunity for them to meet. I was glad Mom wanted to meet Hennie, but once again, that nervous feeling gripped me, making me feel a little awkward, like a teenager introducing his girlfriend to his parents for the first time. Hennie also felt the same way as I did when I asked her to join us for dinner on my birthday. She gladly accepted the invitation, but I could sense her apprehension and trepidation. Women have an innate sense that they are being judged and scrutinized by other women when they first encounter each other. I, too, was a little apprehensive about how they would interact, but I felt it was time that they met. I wanted Hennie to meet Mom and understand my responsibilities associated with her care and why much of my time was committed to her. Hennie was now becoming a part of my life and it was only fair she saw with whom I was sharing it.

The day arrived for my birthday dinner and Mom was all dressed up in her best clothes. She looked elegant and very fashionable. I went to pick up Hennie at her parent's home, and drove her over to my house to meet Mom. Hennie, too, was dressed like a fashion plate: beautiful and elegant. When Hennie and I arrived at my house, Mom was sitting in the living room like a lady in waiting. I made the appropriate introductions and they both exchanged cordialities. We both helped Mom into the car and off we went to Dante's for dinner. Once inside the restaurant, Hennie and Mom started talking about the fashion world; Mom from the designer side, and Hennie from the model side. They talked about styles, fabrics, color, hemlines, and sleeve lengths. Mom was impressed with Hennie's knowledge of the fashion industry, as was Hennie with Mom's. I wasn't able to get a word in edgewise. They went on and on, sharing a commonality that interested them both. I have never seen Mom so animated and excited, her face was glowing and her eyes were twinkling. Hennie, too, was exuberant and excited. I was thrilled that they got along so well and enjoyed each other's company and conversation.

After a beautiful dinner together, we went back to my house and the conversations continued. Mom proceeded to show Hennie some of the dresses that she designed. Hennie was very impressed with Mom's designs and the workmanship that went into them. They were like two little girls playing with dolls, both laughing and energized. Mom was beaming with pride as she showed off her most favorite apparel. I could tell Mom was happy to have met Hennie and share her past experiences with her, but the real final acceptance gesture was when Mom asked me to take out the *Strega* and toast to the wonderful day we all shared together. I was so relieved that they both got along so well. Mom was very gracious and congenial, and Hennie was so pleasant and charming. Hennie always had a smile on her face that lights up a room, and her charismatic and amiable personality enamors her to everyone she meets. My heart was filled with joy as I observed them together. Sharing the day with Mom and Hennie was the best birthday present I could have received.

Hennie worked during the week and usually if I saw her during the week, it would be after work for a late dinner. Since I had to cook for Mom before seeing Hennie, I thought it would be a great idea if she came over and had dinner at my house one evening with Mom and me. Mom and I usually ate dinner in the kitchen, but when she heard that Hennie was coming over, she had me serve dinner in the dining room. Mom was excited that Hennie was coming over; she referred to it as having a party. She got all dressed up and awaited Hennie's arrival. When Hennie arrived, Mom was sitting in the kitchen watching me cook just as she had for the past few years. Hennie was impressed with my cooking skills and Mom elaborated on my abilities as any mother would. I was a little nervous at first, but I soon began to feel comfortable with Hennie there.

When dinner was ready, Hennie escorted Mom to the dining room while I brought the food to the table. Mom sat at the head of the table in her usual spot ever since she and Dad had bought their house. I sat in Dad's spot at the other end and Hennie was seated on the side. Throughout the entire meal, Mom filled Hennie's ears with stories of her life as she so often did at family gatherings. Once again, Mom was very animated and excited as she recalled her past life. I could tell Hennie was genuinely interested in Mom's tales. We shared a pleasant few hours together at dinner with plenty of food and laughter. Mom's acceptance of Hennie in our home was once again solidified with the serving of *Strega!* Hennie and I cleaned up the dinner dishes while Mom retired to the den to watch television. After we were through and I knew Mom was settled in for the night, Hennie and I walked over to the Sly Fox to visit with some friends. It was a very enjoyable evening for both of us and our relationship seemed to take on a new aura.

The dinner parties became a routine several days a week, with Mom and Hennie enthralled in conversation about the fashion world and how each of them had their role. Mom also recanted many other aspects of her life with her unending stories of her life. Hennie knew how important it was for me to take care of my mother and my commitment to her care. She respected what I had to do and she unselfishly shared her time with me. Sharing a few hours with my mother and me was easy for a family-oriented person such as Hennie. Mom was always excited when she knew Hennie was coming over for dinner. She always made sure she was dressed and her hair coiffed and with fresh lipstick on. After all, it was a party!

Hennie and I also continued to go out to restaurants for dinner, but at Hennie's suggestion, we took Mom out with us occasionally. Mom was thrilled to go out with us and felt very special. Hennie would come over before we would go out and help Mom get dressed up. She would help Mom select an outfit and also fix her hair and put her make-up on. It was as if she was dressing up a doll. She fussed over her with a caring and discerning eye, making sure Mom looked prim and proper. Mom enjoyed the attention and was grateful for the assistance. There seemed to be a bonding between the two of them; it was a genuine and gentle caring that was evident by true concern and undaunted respect for each other.

My relationship with Hennie seemed to have catapulted overnight. There was cohesiveness and an interconnected feeling that unified us together. Hennie was now a very important part of my life, filling the void by adding warmth, understanding, support, and love. It was a new beginning for both of us, filled with sharing and love. She elevated me and respected me for the person I was and her compassion and love was selfless. She truly fell from heaven, a person of character and beauty, the object of my love and admiration!

Chapter 13

Expanding Relationships, More "Parties," History Revisited

Mom was doing well and there seemed to be a new vitality to her. I'm sure my uplifted spirits and mood made her feel more at ease and energized. She enjoyed the many dinner parties we had with Hennie and I know she relished the female bonding that the two of them developed. Diana from next door came over a lot for our dinner parties and she too became very fond of Hennie. We all shared good food and plenty of laughter and conversation many nights a week. It seemed like we were one big happy family. We all felt so at ease and comfortable with Hennie's electrifying personality and her beautiful smile and captivating eyes. She lit up the room and made us all feel rejuvenated.

Hennie and I also shared a lot of private time together, talking and getting to know each other. We still went out dancing and enjoyed time with our friends. The two of us were becoming inseparable; we saw each other every day. Our togetherness just seemed so natural and normal. Our time together made us both very happy and seemed to heal the wounds of our past failed relationships. Our relationship filled all the voids that existed in our past and made us appreciate each other in a special and extraordinary way. We were aware of that something special that we shared, and it elated both of us.

Not only was Hennie warm and loving to me, but she generously and sincerely shared her love with Mom and was truly attentive to her needs. She knew of my commitment to Mom and she willingly and freely accepted it and joyfully partook in her care. Mom was very intuitive and astute, and she felt Hennie's genuine concern for her well-being. Mom truly appreciated Hennie's attention and thoughtfulness. Hennie became very special to Mom and she looked forward to her spending time with us. Mom also surmised how I felt about Hennie, and I know she saw the effect she had on me. Mothers have a way of knowing when a son is falling in love. Mom was happy that I was happy and she knew how we all were becoming closer to each other.

As with all romantic relationships, family involvement becomes more and more intricate. Meeting all the members of each other's family and interacting with them in various social and family gatherings makes one feel a little uneasy in the beginning. Since we were both once married before, it became more awkward and uncomfortable.

Hennie had invited me to a family barbeque at her younger sister's home in New Jersey. It was the first time she had brought a date to meet her family since her separation and divorce. We both felt a little uneasy and felt like we were on display and possibly being scrutinized. The trip was too far for Mom to join us, so she spent the day with Tony and Judy, and Hennie and I drove to New Jersey with Hennie's older sister, Hedda, and her boyfriend, Dom. I met Hennie's younger sister, Heidi, and her husband, Bill. They are both radiologists and they live in a beautiful home with a large swimming pool nestled away in a lovely suburban area. They were very hospitable, warm, and friendly. Their three children, Jessica, Michael, and Dana, were all frolicking in the pool with Hedda's daughter, Kasey. Hennie's parents were there also, enjoying the beautiful weather and abundant food.

Hennie has a wonderful, close, warm, and loving family; I felt very comfortable with them. Having had the opportunity to witness Hennie's family interact with each other, it became very apparent to me why Hennie was so loving and warm. When you grow up with love and are surrounded by warm and loving family members, you become a wonderful and caring individual yourself. I was truly enamored and captivated with her whole family. We all spent a lovely day together engaged in eating and stimulating conversation and laughter. When we left to go back to New York, I felt as if I had known Hennie's family for ages.

Mom was doing well and it appeared she was yearning to become somewhat more independent. Even though Mom had made great strides in her physical rehabilitation, she was still a little unsteady when walking. Linda, her healthcare worker, was always by her side during the day when Hennie and I were working. Since Mom was always self-sufficient and independent, I think she felt a little restricted and constrained in her movements, particularly around the neighborhood. She expressed her desire to be a little freer and less guarded. In my desire to make her feel more independent, I purchased a three-wheel walker with hand brakes and a shopping basket. She was able to stroll up and down the driveway and the sidewalk, providing her with exercise as well as stability and security. She would even venture out around the corner to the fruit and vegetable market and buy certain items for the house. She loved her newfound freedom and sense of usefulness. She called her walker a "scooter."

Mom's new sense of independence and having Hennie around added to her wellbeing and contentment. The dinner parties continued and we started including Hennie's family on the weekends. It was one big happy get-together! Mom had a new audience to tell her stories to and I was able to get to know Hennie's family better. I also was able to meet her three children: her twin sixteen-year-old daughters, Jennifer and Christine, and her fourteen-year-old son, Piero.

They were living with Hennie's ex-husband so as not to uproot them from their fine school district and separate them from their friends. Since the crowd of people was larger, Hennie and I prepared the meals together, making sure we had something to please everyone. And, of course, the guests were introduced to *Strega!*

I had a deck built on to the side of the house off the den. It was level with the house and it enabled Mom to be able to sit outside in the spring and summer months without having to climb steps. We often entertained out there when the weather permitted. Hennie, with her expertise for decorating and eye for color, made sure the deck was full of beautiful flowers and plants. Mom loved spending the afternoon on the deck in the fresh air and admiring the flowers. I even installed an electric retractable awning to shade the deck during the hot sunny days. The deck added a completely new living space to our house; everyone enjoyed it. Hennie and I spent many evenings outside on the deck talking and enjoying the mild summer air after Mom went to bed. On the weekends, we often had breakfast outside and lounged around during the day. We always had a big barbeque on Sunday, inviting whoever could come. Diana, from next door, joined us very often, and she became very close and friendly with Hennie's family. They all got along wonderfully.

Hennie and I were pretty much joined at the hip by now. We spent everyday together, as well as the holidays. On several occasions, especially during the cold winter nights, Hennie would sleep over rather than drive home on icy or snow covered roads by herself. Much to our surprise, Mom was delighted to wake up and find that Hennie was there. She had even suggested that I make room upstairs in one of the dressers so Hennie could keep some of her clothes there. This coming from a ninety-three-year-old woman from the old school was surprising. When Mom knew that Hennie had spent the night, she would wake her up for work by ringing a cowbell she had near her bed. When Hennie and I would come down, Mom had breakfast made for all of us. That was her way of entertaining and feeling as if she was still able to cook on her own. Hennie slept over most weekends and we pretty much stayed around the house. During the winter months, we stayed in and sat around the fireplace, nice and cozy, and watched television. At night, we prepared simple yet hearty meals.

It was somewhat difficult and complicated for Hennie and I to get away anywhere by ourselves. On a few occasions, our housekeeper, Celina, would sleep overnight after Linda left for the day, and allow us to grab an overnight getaway to some romantic little Inn not too far from home. Hennie was very understanding and was comfortable with our limited and restricted time alone. It was difficult, to say the least, for me to balance my commitment to my mother and my involvement with Hennie. What really mattered to Hennie and me was that we were together and our time with each other and the time we spent with our families was always quality time. We made the best of it and everyone was happy. Mom, I know, felt lucky and she was always grateful and appreciative of everyone's attention and care giving. The greatest joy and comfort is being surrounded by caring and loving people. Mom was always loving and caring and now she was the recipient of that special gift. One can only paraphrase the old saying, "What goes around, comes around."

Everything was going well in our little comfortable and secure world. Our days were filled with work and our evenings were filled with taking care of Mom and family involvement. Mom required a little more attention due to her advancing age, but her added care was not too burdensome or onerous. She was very content and peaceful, and Hennie and I were at ease with ourselves and our shared duties toward Mom. Peace and tranquility abounded and our lives were unencumbered and worry-free. Life and the world around us were simple and tranquil, and continued on, day after day, season after season. It seemed as if we were in a shell or cocoon, insulated and shielded from any extraneous events that were capable of disrupting our serene way of life.

Tragedy and disaster erupted on September 11, 2001, with the horrific attack on the twin towers of the World Trade Center. Our lives, as well as the lives of the whole world, became traumatized and vulnerable. Fear and trepidation filled every household with anxiety and apprehension. The countless loss of lives and shattered families shrouded our hearts and minds with sorrow and grief. Our once carefree and untroubled existence was taken from us and replaced with uncertainty and insecurity. Mom was confused and shaken by these events and displayed fear and panic. Hennie and I tried to quell her fears and reassure her of her safety. She had lived through many wars and conflicts in her life, and now at this age, she was too frail and fragile to endure the heartaches that come with war and disaster.

Since I am certified in forensic dentistry, I was summoned to the office of the chief medical examiner in New York City to be part of the Dental Identification Unit responsible for identifying the victims of the terrorist attacks. It was a heart-wrenching and difficult duty. That evening, when I returned home, I realized how lucky I was and how fortunate I was to have Hennie in my life. I realized how fragile life was and how tragedy can rob people of their happiness. It became apparent to both of us that the one thing that was lacking in our relationship was the lifelong commitment of marriage. I felt that asking Hennie to marry me would give us both the binding security and love that marriage provides. It would seal our love for one another, enhance our commitment to each other, and establish stability in our lives. It would also provide Mom with a more secure environment.

Our engagement was met with happiness and blessings from our families and friends. Mom was a little reticent in the beginning, thinking that we would leave her for a life on our own. Once she was reassured that nothing would change and that Hennie would move in with us on a permanent basis, she became more secure and at ease with our decision. Hennie and I now felt as if we were one, soul mates embarking on a new chapter in our lives filled with love and commitment. We had direction and purpose, a reason for togetherness, and a goal for life. Everything we did now was as a couple, sharing and giving of ourselves to our families. Hennie's love and caring for Mom took on a new meaning for her. Hennie's love for me was evidenced in her care and devotion to Mom. Mom felt Hennie's genuine love and relentless caring and attention. She welcomed Hennie into her life and her heart.

The family dinners were now more complete; they had a new meaning, the joining of two families as one. There was hope and expectation for Hennie and me. We now acted as a couple rather than two individuals. Not only did we share more things, but also we planned for our future together. After both of us had bad first marriages, we looked forward with anticipation to sharing a beautiful and loving new life together. Yes, it would be slightly encumbered with caring for Mom, but we both were committed to her care and well-being. With maturity, it's easier to sacrifice and give of one's self. Hennie learned how to be loving and caring from her parents, and I learned from mine. Hennie and I entered this new phase of our lives with both eyes wide open, no surprises, and no misgivings. It was a wonderful and beautiful period for us.

With our engagement and future commitments, it was a natural and practical progression for Hennie to move in with Mom and me. It made things easier for all of us. Both Mom and I welcomed Hennie's place in our home, and her full-time presence added a glow to our lives. Not only was she a great homemaker, but she added vibrancy and an electricity to our everyday environment. It was a great comfort to Mom to have Hennie around while I was embroiled in other various activities. There was a sense of belonging and it felt so natural as she fit into our home so well. She also added warmth, style, and charm to our lives. She also benefited from the added space over her apartment. I was delighted with this new phase of our lives; it gave me a sense of security and offered me the closeness and warmth that I had been lacking since my divorce.

Mom started needing more care as time progressed, especially in the evening after her home care attendant left for the day. Hennie became more involved in helping her get ready for bed. She would help her undress and put on her nightclothes, something that was easier for a female to do, rather than a son. On weekends, we did not have anyone taking care of Mom, so Hennie attended to Mom's daily hygiene needs and dressing. Hennie took care of Mom as if she were playing with a doll. She was always pleasant and joking with Mom as she went about her routine. Mom found it amusing and she was always smiling and joking back. Hennie always made sure Mom was properly and fashionably dressed and made up and looking her best. We always involved Mom in everything we did around the house, giving her a sense of belonging and keeping her mentally stimulated. Mom took several short naps during the day, allowing us some free time to attend to our own individual needs.

Mom usually retired for bed shortly after dinner, allowing us a few hours in the evening to spend some time talking and planning our future. Occasionally, Hennie's sister, Hedda, and Dom would come over for a visit. Sundays were usually spent with family coming over for dinner. Hennie and I would spend the morning hours preparing an abundance of food for the "party." Mom was always excited when we told her we were having people over for dinner; she loved the company and loved the attention and fuss everyone made over her. As usual, Mom would amuse her audience with her countless stories of her youth and working career.

In the early spring, while watching the evening news, we learned that Erik Lindbergh, the grandson of Charles Lindbergh, was going to commemorate the seventy-fifth anniversary of his grandfather's historic flight by repeating the journey from New York to Paris on a solo flight. On a capricious whim, I went on the internet and found out the details of the event. There was a section under comments; I wrote in my mother's account of witnessing Lindbergh's landing in Paris and the gala celebrations that ensued. The Lindbergh Foundation promptly responded with the fact that, to the best of their knowledge, Mom was the only living American witness to that historic landing. They notified the producers of The History Channel and within days, they flew to New York, conducted a taped interview of Mom, and verified her story and documents of the event.

On the day Erik Lindbergh was to make his commemorative flight, Mom, Hennie, and I were taken by a chauffeured limousine to the flight area. Mom was so excited and animated; she was like a girl going to her first prom. When we arrived at the flight area, there was a special luncheon set up and all the press and media were present. Mom was bombarded with a rush of reporters from television, radio, and the newspapers. She was treated like royalty. She gave her interview one by one as the media lined up to hear her recounting of that great event. Her interviews were broadcast around the world. Mom was visibly nervous, but she maintained her charm and demeanor like a lady of dignity. She brought with her a small cross that she had purchased as a memento when she was in Paris. She gave it to Erik to ensure his safe flight with God's blessing. After the interviews, we were escorted out to the field and witnessed the takeoff. Mom revisited her special moment in time and it was her true moment of glory. She felt so very special!

A few weeks after Erik's successful and safe flight, Mom was invited to a special dinner celebration commemorating Erik's flight. Once again, Mom was treated like a queen. She was so thrilled to be honored in such a fashion. Once again, the media was enthralled with her stories and she was the center of attention. Mom felt so important and it gave her a new breath of life. A moment in history revisited!

Much of the rest of that spring and summer were spent in preparation of our wedding in October. Mom was thrilled to be part of the planning process. We made her feel important and valued her opinions. We planned a simple and small wedding to include close family and friends. The more we tried to keep it simple, the more and more it became elaborate. It was to be a special day for us and we wanted a simple but elegant wedding. What really mattered to Hennie and me was that we were formally sealing our commitment and love for each other by getting married.

Chapter 14

MARRIAGE, FAMILY UNITY, INTENSIFIED HOME-CARE

Hennie and I were married on a beautiful, sunny October day. Our closest friends and family joined us in our celebration and pledge of love. It was a simple but elegant and beautiful affair. Hennie's two sisters, Hedda and Heidi, were her maids of honor, and my brother, Tony, and my nephew, Anthony, were my best men. Mom was dressed elegantly, as usual, and gave the opening prayer before dinner. It was a wonderful and memorable occasion and a joyous uniting of two fantastic families. We spent a short romantic honeymoon in Italy while Mom stayed with Tony and Judy. Upon our return, our married life began with the normal routine of everyday commitments, and of course, the continued home-care of Mom.

Our frequent family gatherings and holiday celebrations took on a new and special meaning now that we were married. It was one big happy and united family. Mom was still the center of attention with her famous stories and her sweet demeanor. She looked forward to and enjoyed the Sunday dinners and parties. With her increasing age, however, she was showing signs of slowing down and moments of forgetfulness. She started requiring more and more help moving around. Everyone, in his own way, partook in helping her in some manner or fashion. Dom, Hedda's boyfriend, always sat next to Mom at the dinner table, and helped her getting to the table and cutting her food. Mom always responded by looking at Dom with an appreciative and warm loving smile.

Mom was aware of her increasing instability while walking and her increased need for assistance. She was frustrated to a degree, but became receptive to the idea of a walker. It provided her with more stability and a sense of security while walking around the house. At night, she would rely on the walker when she woke up to use the bathroom. We felt more at ease knowing it would help her and prevent a possible fall. Whenever we went out with Mom, we brought her walker with us. She adapted very easily and it helped her to be more mobile and less sedentary. We encouraged her to walk around the house to keep limber and prevent her muscles from becoming atrophied. When she was outside, she exercised with her scooter, strolling up and down the driveway.

Mom's home-care attendant finished her schooling and informed us she was leaving for a hospital position. Mom was upset but understood her need to move on in her career; but for Hennie and me, we were now faced with a dilemma. Mom needed to have someone with her during the day while we were working and out of the house. It was very difficult to find reliable and good help in the home-care sector. Hennie decided to leave her job and take on the full responsibility of taking care of Mom day and night. In the past, we were somewhat restricted and homebound, especially on weekends, but now we were just as homebound as Mom. I was less restricted than Hennie because I still had my work at the office. Hennie, on the other hand, was confined to the house seven days per week and took on all the chores of the house in addition to the responsibility for all of Mom's care. Our only free time was at night when Mom was sleeping; and at that, we had to be vigilant that she was secure in bed.

Our only source of entertainment was having people over for dinner a few times during the week and on weekends. We looked forward to the company and the diversity in our routine. Hennie bore the brunt of the responsibility and care for Mom. She always had a smile on her face and never complained about how intense and difficult it was to attend to all of Mom's needs. Mom was very fortunate to have Hennie taking care of her with such love and warmth. Hennie always made sure Mom was comfortable and clean. She dressed her every day and made sure she looked beautiful and elegant, not like an unkempt old woman. Hennie gave her the respect and dignity she deserved and was used to her whole life. At night, when Hennie had finished changing Mom for bed and making sure she was tucked in for the night, she would call me in to say goodnight. I would lean down, kiss her, and tell her I loved her. She would smile and say, "I love you, too." Then Hennie would do the same and Mom would thank her and tell her she loved her. It was very gratifying to know that we were loved and appreciated by such a special person. In a certain way, we felt like Mom was our child, totally dependent on us for love and all her worldly needs.

I was very fortunate to have Hennie by my side, not only for being the beautiful wife and friend she was to me, but also for being the wonderful and caring person she was to my mother. Everyone remarked and took notice how loving and caring she was toward Mom. One very special person caring for another very special person!

Even though we were limited in our outside activities, we did have a routine that worked well. I would go to work early in the morning and Hennie would be with Mom until I returned home in the late afternoon. I would stay with Mom while Hennie went out and did some minor shopping around the corner. Even though Mom would take several naps during the day, Hennie could not chance leaving her alone for fear of her falling. On the weekends, Hennie would do the major grocery shopping and I would stay with Mom and entertain her as best I could. We were no longer able to go out at night for a few hours as we had in the past because we did not want to take a chance of something happening to Mom. We were content and resigned to our commitment, and we made the best of the situation.

Hennie's parents were well aware of our so-called confinement and lack of outside activities, and occasionally they would call us and say that they would bring over a pizza pie and stay with Mom while we could go to the movies. They would invite Diana over and the four of them would have a pizza party. Mom loved those impromptu dinner parties, and she especially loved her pizza. Helen and Henry were wonderful and thoughtful in-laws and they treated Mom as if she were their mother. They were always gentle and very caring toward Mom. Henry was like the protective son, and Helen was like the sweet and loving daughter. It was a nice break for Hennie and me to sneak away for a few hours, air our minds out, and be entertained a little. Going out to dinner with Mom was now becoming more difficult, but we did manage to take her to Dante's every once in a while as a treat. Mom was definitely slowing down quite a bit and it was best to keep her comfortable and secure in her home environment. Whenever we did take her anywhere, she would always want to return home to her palace after a very short while. We did not want to tire her or make her feel uncomfortable, so we always gave in to her wishes. Her bedtime was now getting earlier and she would sleep later in the morning; that coupled with several daily naps was a sign of her deterioration due to aging.

As simple and routine as Mom's wants and needs were, they still required our full attention twenty-four hours a day. We had to be constantly vigilant and cautious in our handling of her. We took care of feeding her, dressing her, cleaning her, dispensing her medications, putting her to bed, and keeping her as alert as possible. She was always very comfortable and never complained about anything. She was quite content and happy. She spent a lot of time in the den in her recliner watching television. When the weather was nice, we would bring her out on the deck and she would enjoy looking at the flowers and watching the birds and squirrels ramble around the backyard. She would often doze off for a short nap while enjoying the pleasant warm breeze of the spring air. Many evening meals were served on the deck for a change of pace during the spring and summer months.

The Sunday family dinners continued, but Mom started to become less and less communicative and outgoing, and would just sit there with an observant smile and quietly listen to the conversations and joking around the table. Everyone at the table would try to include her in the conversations, but Mom would only respond briefly with a few words and a gentle and placid smile. Her appetite also started to diminish over time and we had to encourage and persuade her to finish her meals. It was a special challenge for us to maintain her nutrition and hydration. Mom always had a sweet tooth, and often times we would coax and cajole her into finishing her meal by showing her a box of chocolates or an assortment of pastries. Helen and Henry always brought over a tempting box of dessert when they came for dinner. At times, she acted like a little girl, all bright-eyed and smiling when the dessert came to the table. Elderly people start to revert back to childhood in many respects; probably one of the good things about aging.

Day after day, week after week, and month after month flew by, and our care and maintenance of Mom became more and more intensified. Early stages of dementia were setting in and it was sad to see Mom deteriorate in such a way. She was always sharp and alert, and now she was forgetful and losing touch with reality. There were times when she would forget her age, name, and who we were. We made light of her forgetfulness and would joke around with her. Nevertheless, deep inside of me, my heart was breaking to see the once pillar of strength of our family become so frail and feeble. All we could do was nurture her and protect her and make sure that she was comfortable. Hennie had the brunt of the burden of taking care of Mom, yet it was taking a toll on both of us. When you are motivated by love and a sense of duty, you rise to the occasion and no task is insurmountable.

No matter how cautious and vigilant we thought we were being, an accident could and did happen. Mom was napping in the den one Saturday, late in the afternoon, and Hennie and I were in the kitchen preparing for our usual Sunday family dinner. We heard a loud noise and felt a heavy vibration from the den.

We ran into the den and saw Mom lying on the floor with her head against the fireplace. Apparently, she had woken from her nap and attempted to get up and reach for her walker. She must have tripped or lost her balance and fell forward. She was bleeding profusely from her head and she was unresponsive and limp. Hennie called 911 while I applied pressure to her head to stop the bleeding. Hennie also called her parents to apprise them of the situation. Hennie rode with Mom in the ambulance along with the paramedics and I followed in my car. Mom was swiftly and competently attended to in the emergency room of the hospital. She required several sutures to her scalp and a few staples. She was conscious in the emergency room, but very confused and scared.

Mom was admitted to the hospital for observation and precautionary measures due to her age. I felt so helpless and powerless; I was not in control of her welfare at that moment and I became frightened and scared. I started to feel culpable for Mom's accident and questioned my competence as a caregiver. Hennie and her parents reassured me that there was no way to predict or prevent such an unfortunate accident from occurring. Nonetheless, I felt responsible and upset that Mom was injured and hospitalized. Mom was released from the hospital after a few days, and for some reason, she was totally unaware of what had happened to her. She knew she was sore on top of her head, but she had no recollection of the fall and her stay in the hospital. We told her she had a slight fall and bruised her head.

It became very apparent to us now that it was time for us to have some outside help since Mom required constant side-by-side care. There was no way that Hennie or I could be by her side every waking moment of the day. We could not take the chance that Mom would try to get up and walk without our supervision and control. As an added precaution, we had bedrails installed on her bed so we could be rest assured she would not get up and walk around by herself late at night or early in the morning.

Finding someone to be by Mom's side constantly was an arduous and time-consuming task. We interviewed several people and we were very fortunate to find a wonderful woman who had immigrated to this country a few years ago from Poland. Her name was Lucy, and she was a caring and responsible person. She took care of Mom from 9 a.m. until 3 p.m. Monday through Friday, allowing Hennie the time to take care of the other household chores that needed to be done. Hennie and I took over watching Mom when Lucy left for the rest of the day and night. Mom became very fond of Lucy, as they were side-by-side most of the time. We felt very comfortable and relieved that Mom was in very good and reliable hands. Even when Mom was napping, Lucy was nearby making sure she was comfortable and securely safe in her recliner. She would hold Mom's arm securely while Mom strolled with her walker, making sure Mom did not stumble or lose her balance. We became very reliant on Lucy to give us the help we so desperately needed.

The weekends were rough for us without Lucy, but as before, we managed to make the best of it and with the occasional help from Hennie's parents, it was relatively uneventful. Mom was used to having Lucy with her all the time and she had a difficult time understanding why she was not there in the evenings and on weekends. Mom had lost all perspective of time and days, and was confusing daytime with nighttime. She even started forgetting who Hennie and I were, calling both of us Lucy. When we would tell her that Lucy had left for the day, she would look at us with a perplexed and bewildered stare. After a few minutes, Mom would forget about Lucy, relax, and watch television. She would go to bed shortly after dinner and sleep comfortably through the night.

Very often, when I would come home from work and go over to Mom when she was relaxing in the den, she would not recognize me when I leaned down to kiss her. She would look up at me with an inquisitive stare and ask who I was. When I told her I was her son Dennis, she would glean a faint sweet smile on her face and ask if she could kiss me. I would lean down and she would give me a soft loving kiss on my cheek and tell me she loved me. She would then take my hand in hers and gently squeeze it in a loving and warm way. Even in her moments of confusion and episodes of dementia, Mom was always sweet, loving, warm, and docile. It broke my heart to see her so confused at times, but her warm and loving manner overcame my disenchantment with her dementia and advancing age.

Our being house-bound most of the time was starting to take its toll on Hennie and me. We decided to have Lucy stay with Mom on Saturday evenings from six until ten, feed her dinner, and put her to bed so that we could go out for dinner and little a socializing with some friends. It was therapeutic and a much needed break from our isolation. When we came home at night, Mom was fast asleep and had not even known we were gone for those few hours. The next morning, it was back to our normal routine, but Hennie and I were refreshed and energized from our brief escape from the night before.

Since I was required to take continuing education courses in order to maintain my license as a dentist in New York, it was difficult for me to obtain the amount of hours needed while being limited by caring for Mom. With the help of Lucy and Hennie's parents, Hennie and I were able to arrange to attend certain dental conventions out of town. Lucy would take care of Mom during the daytime, and then Helen and Henry would stay with Mom after she left. They would sleep over and keep a watchful eye over Mom until Lucy came back the next morning. Mom was well taken care of and entertained while we were away. They would invite Diana over from next door and they would have little dinner parties as a distraction for Mom. Hennie and I combined business with pleasure and were able to have a well-needed, short vacation. I felt very at ease and comfortable knowing that Mom was in such competent and loving hands. Their help and love were well appreciated.

While away, I would call every evening and talk to Mom. Not really having any concept of time, she thought I was at work and would be home shortly. I placated her by telling her I would be home in an hour or two. She quickly forgot that she even spoke to me and would go about her normal routine. If she knew we were going away for any length of time, she might have panicked or felt abandoned. When we came home from our trip, Mom was sleeping and the next morning was like any other morning; she never knew we were gone. We were not trying to deceive her, we were only trying to protect her and prevent her from having any unnecessary fear or anxiety. Our constant goal was Mom's safety and peace of mind. In her weak and frail condition, we felt it best never to give her any reason to be alarmed or frightened. We always tried to keep bad news and unpleasant situations from her.

One very sad and upsetting event that we kept from Mom was Tony and Judy's decision to move from New York to a warmer climate in the south. For them, retiring to the south afforded them a healthier and more comfortable lifestyle. With the long winters in the north, and the hectic and burdensome congestion of Long Island, it was not a desirable place to spend one's retirement. They would call Mom on the phone and she thought they were home in New York; she never knew they moved so far away. It was a major life-changing decision for them, their children, and their grandchildren, but one that was best-suited and necessary for them. They drove back up to New York for the holidays and special occasions, spending some time with family and friends. If Mom had known of their move, she would have become despondent and depressed. Her whole family during her entire life was mostly centered in and around the New York area. As long as Tony and Judy were in phone contact with her, she was content and not worried. Any separation from family at this delicate stage of her life would be devastating and have an adverse effect on her health. Once again, our main concern was Mom's welfare and peace of mind.

Chapter 15

HEART-WRENCHING DECISIONS, NEVER SAY NEVER

While much of our routine remained the same, Mom was declining in her ability to move around, even with assistance. She was becoming less able to use the walker unless someone held her arms and gave her support. Her legs were becoming weaker and her arms were not strong enough to help support her. She was unable to get up from her recliner by herself; we had to hold onto her hands and pull her up. Once she was up, she was very unsteady and unsure of her footing. Mom would spend most of the day in her recliner, except when we brought her to the bathroom and into the kitchen for her meals. Occasionally, we would bring her out on the front porch or the deck for a change of scenery. Lucy never left her side and would firmly hold onto her every step she took. It was becoming very difficult to provide Mom with the exercise she needed to keep her circulation going and preventing her muscles from atrophying. Mom never complained about her inability to move around on her own. She was very stoic and accepting of her ageing and dependence upon others.

It was next to impossible to get Mom into the bathtub and sit her down on the shower seat, even though we had handrails installed in order for her to support herself. Mom could not raise her legs to climb into the tub and it was too difficult to lift her. We were fearful she might slip on the wet surface and fall. Hennie and Lucy had to resort to giving Mom sponge baths. It was not the ideal way to bathe Mom, but it was the best that they could do, given the circumstances. They were very thorough and systematic in their washing of Mom, making sure she was hygienic and sanitary. Mom would sit on the toilet seat quietly and calmly as they attended to her needs. Once she was all clean and dry, they would fix her hair, put her make-up on, dress her in a fresh housecoat, and bring her back in the den for a short nap. It was an arduous routine, but a necessary one for her well-being and hygiene. Mom was always kept meticulously clean and comfortably dressed.

We still managed to have people over for dinner a few times per week, mainly as a diversion for Mom. She seemed to brighten up a little when people were around. Even though she was more placid and less involved in conversation, she gave the appearance that she was enjoying herself. We tried to make it a party atmosphere with an abundance of food and an assortment of tasty desserts. Her appetite was greatly diminished, but she did enjoy the taste of her food, especially the desserts. Her eyes would really light up when I gave her a small glass of *Strega* with her dessert. She would look at me with a tiny smile and raise her glass as if she were toasting to me. Even at her level of forgetfulness and advancing dementia, I was certain that the taste and aroma of the *Strega* sparked very warmhearted and pleasant memories for her.

During the daytime hours, when Lucy was there with Hennie, it was somewhat easier to attend to Mom's needs. When Lucy would leave for the day, then it became more of a challenge for Hennie to manage on her own. I tried as best I could to help with some of the care, but Hennie bore the brunt of the responsibilities involved, especially Mom's hygiene needs. Hennie had a well-organized and systematic routine that catered to Mom's every need and insured her well-being and safety. Hennie's sense of duty and obligation never wavered nor became slipshod. Not only was Hennie meticulous in her actions, but she performed her duties in a pleasant and tender way. She never let Mom sense that she was in any way a burden or too difficult to manage. I'm sure Mom realized how much attention she needed and how loving and devoted Hennie was to her. Mom always smiled and was content when Hennie was tending to her. Hennie always joked around with Mom and tried to make the tasks seem like a game to her.

As time progressed, it was becoming increasingly more difficult to assist Mom around the house. We decided to purchase a lightweight wheelchair from a local medical supply store. I thought Mom would vehemently oppose being in a wheelchair because it would make her feel like she was an invalid. Quite to our surprise, she liked her new chair and the way it enabled her to get around the house without the strain of walking. I think I had a harder time adjusting than Mom. I looked upon it as another step closer to her total decline and deterioration. I was saddened and upset to see her so frail and unable to do anything except sit and be wheeled around. The wheelchair did relieve the physical burden for us, but nonetheless, all the other responsibilities still required great fortitude and stamina. The one thing I feared the most was the fact that being in a wheelchair would hasten the atrophy of Mom's muscles and lead to circulation problems. In order to avoid these problems, we added a routine of leg exercises for Mom and daily massages. Mom loved the pampering and soothing effects of the massages, but she was not too fond of the exercises.

Fortunately, both the front porch and back deck were level with the floor of the rest of the house. It made it very easy for us to transport Mom outside for some fresh air when the weather was nice outside. We were even able to be adventuresome and take Mom out to a restaurant from time to time. The only difficult part of taking Mom out was helping her down the few steps to the driveway and lifting her into the car. Taking Mom out proved to be exciting for her and she appeared to enjoy the change of surroundings. It was an adventure for her and a pleasant reprieve from the mundane routine and isolation for Hennie and me.

Mom was generally in a good mood and very accepting of her limited mobility and activities. During the late afternoon, she would sometimes get a little agitated and confused. Sundown syndrome, as it is called, seems to affect the elderly around 4 p.m. . They tend to become disoriented and perplexed, not knowing where they are and fearful of their surroundings. At times, it was very difficult to reassure Mom that everything was alright and that we were there to take care of her. She acted sometimes like a child afraid of the night and being left alone. Many times, when I was at the office, I would receive a call from Hennie asking me to talk to Mom to reassure her I was all right and that I would be home shortly. She was always fearful that something had or would happen to me; much like a child who worries about losing his parents. Her fears and worries were all part of the aging process and we had to use many psychological skills to deal with her.

We tried as best we could to manage all of the ever-increasing demands related to Mom's advancing age. As time progressed, Mom was becoming more and more debilitated and confused. She was always asking us if the room she was in was her house. She would peruse her surroundings and have a bewildered look on her face, as if she were there for the first time. I would have to point out familiar objects or pictures of family members to reassure her that this was her home. She would look at me with disbelief and question me for the truth. After awhile, she would finally become somewhat reassured and at peace. The only area in the house that she really was familiar with was her sleeping area. She was always fond of leopard prints as a designer; all her bedding and the surrounding areas had leopard prints and designs. It was her comfort zone and we elaborated on it with all sorts of pillows and stuffed animals in leopard print. Even her favorite nightgown had a leopard print pattern.

Mom's bouts with incontinence became constant as time progressed. Hennie and Lucy were always changing Mom several times during the day. At night, Hennie would use double diapers to help keep her dry and comfortable. Many times during the night, Mom would ring her bell that we had at her bedside to alert us of her need to go to the bathroom. We had to literally sleep with one eye open and an alert ear so we could respond to her calls, no matter what time of night it was. Mom had no real idea of day and night, and she never realized the hour, no matter how late it was. She confused her days and nights very often. When we would bring her into the kitchen for dinner, she would say good morning, as if she were coming in for breakfast. At times, we had to convince her that it was late at night and that it was past her bed time. We tried as best we could to keep her familiar with the time of day so she would not feel disoriented with night and day. The fact that she napped very often during the daytime added to her disorientation of time, but it was impossible to prevent her from her frequent napping. The fact that she napped so often during the day was indicative of her heart slowing down and her brain not getting enough blood supply, a very common occurrence with advancing age.

At times, I felt that I had a harder time adjusting to Mom's deteriorating condition than she did. In some respects, I put it out of my mind, hoping that things would get better as time went by. I guess you could say that I was in denial, and not wanting to accept or deal with the inevitable and unavoidable reality of life and death. I tried to repress my true emotions and hold back my acceptance of facing the foreseeable future. Caring for and protecting Mom carried the same responsibilities and love as raising a child. The difference between the two is that at some point, a child becomes less dependent and reliant; they mature and go on in life and flourish. Mom, on the other hand, was declining and waning on a path to a final demise. It hurt immensely to witness the day-to-day deterioration and weakening of a loved one. The future holds only pain and unhappiness as the aging process continues. All I could do was to try to enrich her final days as best I could, and endow her with all the love and enjoyment that was obtainable.

Everyone around us saw the strain that Hennie and I were under. They knew how intense our routine hard work was to care for Mom. Their accolades and praise were well appreciated; however, they were more realistic and pragmatic than Hennie and I. They were able to be more objective than we were, and foresee the inevitable anguish that was imminent. My attentiveness to Mom was motivated by my deep love and sense of duty and commitment to her. Hennie's attentiveness was motivated by her love for Mom and her devotion, love, and respect for me. Together we were embroiled in an undertaking that clouded our realistic outlook of the future. Everyone was very supportive and understanding of us and empathetic to our plight. They saw how difficult it was at times to deal with Mom's complex and intricate needs. Their presence and encouragement during the family gatherings helped immensely. Sometimes when you are going through a difficult period in your life, having understanding and loving people around you lessens the burden to some degree.

Hennie and I stayed close to home more now that Mom was weakening; we wanted to be close at hand in case of any sudden emergencies or unforeseen accidents that might occur. Hennie's parents offered to watch Mom to give us a weekend break; we felt it would be selfish of us to go away and burden them with that responsibility, even though they were very capable of taking care of her. Both Hennie and I would not be able to relax and enjoy ourselves for fear that anything would happen to Mom while we were away. Other people may have done things differently and been more concerned with their own happiness, but I was less concerned with my own pleasures than I was with Mom's wellbeing and safety. She was my foremost priority and I would not put my own needs above her needs; especially now, in her frail and delicate condition. Call it being over-protective, but I was the only one who was ultimately accountable for Mom's welfare. I never wanted to open myself up to criticism or leave room for anyone to cast blame on me for anything that would happen to Mom due to any alleged neglect.

As the weeks and months went by, I noticed Mom's alertness and coherence rapidly declining. Her doctor reassured me that medically she was stable and only needed closer monitoring, but that her dementia was progressing. We all concentrated our efforts to maintain our care for Mom in a methodical and meticulous manner as best we could. Certain doubts kept entering my thoughts as to how well our efforts were working. Outside influences from close friends and family kept alluding to the fact that Mom might benefit more from the help of some skilled nursing care. They suggested that around-the-clock nursing care would greatly relieve us of the necessary duties required to sustain Mom and also provide her with safer and more reliable medical monitoring. I explored the possibilities of hiring nurses during the night hours, but it was next to impossible to arrange. Another suggestion was considering the possibly of placing Mom in a skilled nursing facility.

The mere thought of placing Mom in a nursing home upset and disturbed me immensely. All the years I spent taking care of Mom were part of my profound commitment and promise to her, based upon my love for her as my mother, that I would always take care of her and protect her. To renege on that promise now would destroy my honor and self-respect. Mom depended on me and trusted me all these years; her sense of security was based on her being confident in the fact that I would always be faithful and loving toward her. She was free of worry and at peace in her own home knowing that I was always there caring for her. She knew that everything I did in her home was for her betterment and enrichment. It was total trust, because she knew how committed I was to her care and how much I loved her. For me to violate that trust was reprehensible.

Hennie and I managed over the next few months to continue to keep Mom comfortable and healthy. I spent more time at home and worked less at the office in order to assist Hennie and Lucy with Mom's care as much as I could. Mom was physically stable, but mentally out of touch with her surroundings. It was difficult for us most of the time to communicate with her and elicit any type of coherent response. She did, however, vacillate back and forth with a few lucid moments. Her demeanor was always pleasant and placid; I could tell she was comfortable and contented. She never got agitated or fearful of her surroundings because she sensed the love and attention we were giving her. That was the best we could expect from her and we were grateful that she was so easy-going and easy to manage. Even though my heart was breaking because Mom did not know who I was most of the time, I was able to express my love for her and savored the memory of who she was—the mother who raised me and showered me with an abundance of love her whole life. I looked upon her as the same person who, in my mind, epitomized the essence of a loving and devoted mother. Just because the years had robbed her of her ability to show her love, time cannot erase the loving person she was to so many. It is the person you are caring for who sustains you and fuels your commitment.

First and foremost in my mind were always doing the right thing and the best thing for Mom. I always felt that as long as I was in charge and helping take care of her; it was the best thing for her. I was giving her the best of everything and all the attention and help I could. Seeing her now, and trying to provide what was right for her at this stage of her life started raising doubts in my mind. Was I really doing what was best for her, or was I blinded by my own desire to hold on to her and possibly deny her the proper skilled care that was available in a nursing home? Was I selfish or was I afraid of failure or too stubborn to admit I was no longer capable of being a caregiver? Guilt started setting in when I entertained thoughts that I was possibly not doing what was best for Mom. With the exception of Hennie, everyone was advising me that I needed to seriously consider placing Mom in a nursing home and allow her better access to twenty-four-hour skilled care.

The big question and hard decision that I was faced with was what was the best thing for Mom. For me to reconcile in my own mind this life-altering decision was a painful and heart-wrenching choice. After weeks of sleepless nights and ponderous days, I finally came to the painful realization that placing Mom in a nursing home was, in fact, the best thing that I could do for her; and by doing so, I would be living up to my promise of taking care of her. I was relinquishing only my physical and proximate care of her, not my pledge to provide the best for her. Sometimes letting go and delegating to other people what you are no longer qualified to do turns out to be the best thing for someone you love. I always remember Mom telling me about the difficult choices she had to make in life and how many times you have to be level-headed and strong and forget what your heart tells you.

Before committing to any final decision on placing Mom in a nursing home, Hennie and I went out to explore various places in our vicinity. We physically inspected all the facilities in-depth, and scrupulously interviewed the nursing and administrative staffs of several nursing homes. On the exterior, they were only slightly different, offering minor variations as to the façade and the landscaping. On the inside, they all presented the same mundane and plain appearance. Overcrowding and understaffing seemed to be the common theme. The rooms left a lot to be desired as far as neatness and décor; they were small, minimally furnished, and poorly ventilated. The hallways were cluttered with leftover food carts and linen baskets. The residents, as the patients are called, were all herded into one common area sitting in wheelchairs and just left there, mostly on their own. Their faces were expressionless and their clothing disheveled and stained. There was a certain noxious odor that permeated the air, indicative of a lack of proper or well-maintained hygiene. All the facilities we visited gave the appearance of disarray and disorder. Both Hennie and I were greatly disappointed and upset to see how senior citizens are forced to spend their final days in such an unpleasant and repulsive atmosphere.

Having witnessed personally the substandard living conditions available in the area nursing homes, I vehemently opposed any further discussion of placing Mom in one. I would not subject her to that kind of life no matter how advanced her dementia or no matter how much she was out of touch with her surroundings. She deserved the best and nothing less. I informed my brother of my findings and told him I would not under any circumstances relinquish my care of Mom. He agreed with me after hearing the deplorable conditions that Mom would have to live in if we put her in a facility in New York. The expense was outrageous and unwarranted for the conditions and the services provided. Reiterating the need to place Mom in a nursing home, he offered to investigate the possibility of relocating Mom down south near where he and Judy were living. It was his understanding, from accounts of friends and neighbors, that there were very beautiful, modern, clean, and efficient facilities in his area, and significantly less expensive than up north. I agreed to let him explore that option, but I was not happy with the idea of not having Mom close to me.

Tony and Judy found a place very close to their home. Hennie and I flew down to inspect the nursing home and we were very pleasantly surprised. It was a modern facility located close to the ocean and nestled amongst tall palm trees and colorful tropical flowers. The inside areas were immaculately clean and beautifully decorated, giving the appearance of private hotel. The bedrooms were spacious and airy with a private bath and sitting area. The air smelled clean and fresh. The abundant nursing staff and attendants were neatly attired and very professional. The dining area gave the appearance of a restaurant with linen tablecloths and napkins. Everything about the place was in sharp contrast to what we saw back home. There were only about thirty residents living there without being crowded or huddled together. I knew immediately that this would be the best place for Mom.

Hennie and I returned to New York and prepared ourselves for the unpleasant undertaking of planning Mom's journey and separation from us. We had to do what was best for Mom, and no matter how much it hurt, we had to let go. Part of loving someone is knowing when to let go. The mental anguish was paralyzing me and my heart was breaking; part of me was being torn away.

Chapter 16

THE PAIN OF SEPARATION—A TIME TO SAY GOOD-BYE

Making the final arrangements to place Mom into a nursing home was easy compared to me mentally accepting her departure. For the past eight years, she had been such an important part of my life. Taking care of her had become a habitual thing that had engulfed my every waking hour. Her presence in this home had kept alive all the wonderful memories of my life as a child growing up and as an adult sharing her life. She loved her home so much and loved entertaining people in her home and making them happy. To have her leave her "palace" now would leave a gaping hole in my life and I would only have the memories of her presence to comfort my loss. Sharing her life for all those years living with her and caring for her had enriched my life immensely. Even though Mom had no idea of what was happening around her and that she would soon be leaving her home, the guilt and anguish were building up in me. How would I deal with the awesome task required of me? How would I reconcile the guilt and deal with the consequences of tearing her away from her life-long residence.

Everyone was distraught by Mom's impending departure. Lucy, who for the past few years had grown to love and admire Mom, was deeply saddened. Diana, who had loved Mom for sixty-three years as a neighbor and dear friend, was extremely upset. Hennie's family became very attached to Mom over the years and they too were all saddened by Mom leaving. Hennie, who was so intimately and completely involved with Mom's care and gave her so much love and respect, was suffering from her own emotions. Everyone who knew and loved her was expressing their own sense of loss in a multitude of ways. Mom had a unique way of touching everyone's hearts and enriching their lives. Even though they all realized that her moving to a nursing home was the best alternative for her, they wished that she could be around them forever.

Since I had the legal power of attorney over my mother's estate, it was relatively easy to handle the complex paper work involved in her admittance to the nursing home.

Every time I signed a release form or a financial document for Mom's admittance to the nursing home, my hands shook and my heart ached. What bothered me the most was that Mom was clueless to the fate I was sealing with my signature. I felt like I was judge, jury, and executioner over my mother's destiny. I spent many a sleepless night pondering my actions and questioning this very life-concluding decision. My heart was heavy and my mind was troubled. As the days drew nearer to Mom leaving, I was beginning to second guess my decisions and attempted to avoid the issue entirely. There was no escaping the grim reality at that point; there was no way out and I had to force myself to fight off my emotions and take control of the situation. Hennie was my pillar of strength, she was very supportive and helped me foster up the courage to stay focused on my undertaking. She was my soul mate and felt and sensed my every emotion and feeling deep within her heart.

As a gesture of support, my brother flew up a few days before transporting Mom down south to be of assistance if needed. Mom did not recognize Tony right away; it took quite a few minutes to convince her that he was her son. As sad as that was, in a way, it was good that she was having difficulty remembering things. Hopefully it would make her transition easier if she was confused as to where she was going or who the people were at the nursing home. None of us were looking forward to what lay ahead of us during the next few days. We were most fearful of her realizing what was happening to her and concerned that her reaction might spark an emotional turmoil that would be detrimental to her physically and mentally. I knew I did not have the emotional strength to deal with forcing her out of her home against her wishes. We were preparing for the worst and hopeful for the best.

Hennie and I planned a special dinner the night before Mom's departure. We had a small crowd of family and friends, all of whom wanted to see her one last time in her home. My nephew, Anthony, came down from Connecticut to join in the farewell dinner. Diana from next door, Hennie's parents, and her sister, Hedda, along with Dom, all came to share one last festivity at our house in honor of Mom. Everyone knew that this was Mom's last dinner party that she would be having with friends and family except her. I prepared one of Mom's favorite meals, *pasta e fagioli,* with a lackluster enthusiasm, because I knew it was the last time I would be cooking for my mother. During the dinner, we kept the conversation light and tried to be as cheery as possible, but there was a somber mood hovering over our heads and a solemn quaking in our hearts. Mom sat in her usual place at the head of the table as she had done so many times for the past sixty-three years. As I looked at her, all the years and hundreds of dinner parties that she hosted flashed before my eyes. There she was, unbeknownst to her, presiding over her last family celebration. At the end of dinner, we all toasted to Mom with a glass of *Strega,* honoring her and her legacy. Tears swelled up in my eyes as I looked into her eyes while she, the Queen, sipped her *Strega* for the last time in her palace.

At the end of the evening, everyone said their

good-byes to Mom in their own special way. It was a morose farewell filled with held-back tears and quivering voices. Mom was not aware of the sadness that filled their hearts. After our guests left, Hennie prepared Mom for bed in her usual loving and meticulous way. When Mom was ready, I leaned over and tenderly kissed her good night as I had done for the past eight years. It was the last time I would be tucking her in for the night and making sure she was comfortable and resting in bed. It was also the last time I would see her with that loving and grateful smile looking back at me. I wished her a good night's sleep and told her I loved her, and she, in her little girlish way, wished me the same. The tears were flowing down my cheek as I closed the light by her bed and left. The stark reality of this being my last goodnight ritual, and the fact that I would no longer be in charge of Mom's welfare, left me with a sense of helplessness and impotence.

After Mom was settled in for the night, Hennie, my brother, and I sat outside on the deck that evening trying to relax and vaporize the vision from our minds of the doleful events that were to take place the following morning; each of us silently wishing the day away. There was no escaping our resolve; it was, after all, the best thing for Mom. We were all exhausted from the tumultuous vacillations of our emotions and the draining events of the last family gathering with Mom. Hennie and Tony retired to bed early so as to be rested for the next morning's ordeal. I sat in a chair nearby where Mom was peacefully sleeping, as if keeping a vigil over her. So many thoughts were racing through my mind, as if I were on a rollercoaster ride; my whole life with her, from childhood through adulthood, flashed by like mini episodes on film. I did not want to let go and I could not hold back the dawn or the hour of her leaving. Time ceases for no one.

The sun rose and my heart sank; it was the morning I had been dreading to deal with for months. Hennie dressed Mom in the usual fashion, only this time she outfitted her in an ensemble suitable for travel. While I sat in the kitchen with Mom as she ate her breakfast, Hennie was busy finishing up the final packing of Mom's clothes. Hennie also packed a suitcase full of all the paraphernalia that surrounded Mom's sleeping area. It was our intent to decorate Mom's private room with all the things that were familiar to her in order to make her new surroundings recognizable. We included all of her leopard fabric bedding, framed family pictures, nightstand items, and even her favorite stuffed animals that she had collected over the years. While Hennie was finishing up with the last minute details of Mom's packing, I sat with Mom, silently staring at her frail figure and trying to hold back the tears that were swelling in my eyes.

The car service that we had arranged to take us to the airport arrived on schedule. As we wheeled Mom to the side door, she expressed happiness in the fact that she was going out for the day. Little did she realize it was her last journey from her home, never to return again. Hennie and I sat on either side of Mom in the back seat, I grasping Mom's hand as the car pulled away from our house. As we drove down our street, Mom had a pleasant smile on her face as she glanced at the familiar houses along the way. She was totally unaware that this was the last time she would see the neighborhood that she and Dad had so enthusiastically pioneered over sixty years ago. As I held Mom's hand, I was wrought with the haunting feeling that I was, in all actuality, kidnapping her from her home. I had to constantly reinforce in my mind that what I was doing was the only right and acceptable means of making sure Mom was well taken care of and protected from any harm.

While at the airport, Mom sat in her wheelchair with a placid, inquisitive smile on her face as she glanced around the waiting area observing all the people. She was oblivious as to where she was and what was going on around her. I had arranged first class seating in the first row for Mom so it would be more spacious and easier for her to be boarded on the plane. While in flight, she just sat there, staring at the front of the compartment, observing the flight attendants going about their assigned duties. I sat next to her, holding her hand the entire trip. She closed her eyes for a brief nap as she had done so many times while at home. As I stared out the plane window, a sudden calm came over me as I glanced at the passing clouds below. The gentle motion of the plane had a tranquilizing effect on me as it glided toward its final destination. I was grateful that Mom, so far, had no ill effects from the trip or suspicions as to what was really happening to her.

We were met at the airport by Judy and her girlfriend, Renee, and her husband, Julie. They all were there to help assist us with transporting Mom and her luggage to the nursing home, which was a short drive away. When we arrived at the nursing home, we wheeled Mom inside directly to the dining room where we had previously arranged for Mom to have lunch. While Mom ate her lunch, Hennie and a few of the attendants unpacked Mom's clothes and set her private room up almost exactly as her sleeping area was at home. Everything fit in beautifully, just as it did at home. When Mom finished her lunch, we suggested that she go to her room to take a nap. She was tired and she willingly agreed that it was a good idea. We wheeled her to her room and as she entered, a serene smile appeared on her face, as if she were content and comfortable with her familiar surroundings. I kissed her on her forehead and she quickly closed her eyes dozing off for a nap.

We all left to go grab a quick bite to eat and relax from our short but emotionally charged journey. When we returned to the nursing home, Mom was sitting up in her wheelchair watching television in the lounge area. She appeared rested and relaxed. We spent a few hours with her and we were amazed that she had no inkling that she was not in her own home; she appeared peaceful and content. After dinner, we spent a little while with her before she was to retire for the night. We were a little concerned that Mom might find it unusual that Hennie did not prepare her for bed. To our surprise,

Mom was undisturbed by being changed by the attendants. We kissed her goodnight as we always had done in the past, and told her we would see her in the morning. It was a very uncomfortable and unsettling feeling leaving Mom alone in a strange place without us there to watch over her. I was despondent and downhearted when we left to spend the night at Tony and Judy's house, which was only a few minutes away from the nursing home.

The next morning, I awoke at the crack of dawn from an uneasy and restless sleep. Hennie and I were to leave to go back to New York after seeing Mom and saying good-bye. I could not bear the thought of leaving her and not being an integral part of her life anymore. I did not know how to let go and relegate her care to others; I was unable to come to grips with my emotions and act accordingly. Somehow, I gathered up the strength and we went to the nursing home early enough to be there while Mom was having breakfast. When we arrived, Mom was sitting at the table in the dining room all dressed up in a beautiful housecoat eating breakfast with some other women. She appeared oblivious to the fact that there were strangers sitting with her. Her hair was neatly coiffed and she had her make-up on. She looked spry and well-rested. I went over to her and kissed her good morning, just as I had done when she was home. She responded with her usual amiable smile and returned my kiss. I was surprised to see Mom looking so alert and seemingly well-adjusted. I watched her as she ate her breakfast with an enthusiastic and fervent appetite.

We spent a few quiet hours with her, holding and stroking her hands before we had to leave for the airport. Knowing that Tony and Judy would visit her during our absence, and that Mom would be disoriented and think it was Hennie and I, eased the fear for us that she would feel abandoned when she did not see us for any long period of time. Hopefully, in her mental condition, she would adapt to her new surroundings and the schedules at the nursing home without any repercussions. We had to catch our flight back home and it was time to leave; there was once again no holding back the clock. I was quivering as I kissed Mom good-bye and told her that I loved her, and said that I had to go to work and that I would see her later, just as I had done so many times back home. She smiled and kissed me back and nodded as if she understood. As we turned to leave, a sudden sinking feeling gripped my heart and throat as if a vice were choking me. My eyes swelled up with tears and my hands shook. My heart was breaking and I was emotionally distraught. Mom was no longer in my care and I would forever be deprived of her loving presence and her gentle tenderness.

On the plane ride home, Hennie and I sat quietly and forlornly, holding each other's hand. At that point, I was more wrapped up in my own emotions than worrying about Mom being taken care of in the nursing home. I knew she would be well cared for with all the attention given by the nursing staff and the close supervision by the doctors. It was the finality of the separation and the lamenting thoughts of the life-altering conclusion to Mom's reliance on me that consumed my mind and tore at my heart. Entering the house after our flight was extremely difficult. Her absence was immediately felt by both of us. The spirit that once filled the house with love and dedication to family and friends was replaced with a barren and blank chill that radiated throughout the rooms. Walking by the now-empty areas where Mom had spent most of her time cast stillness and a quietness that provided evidence that a once vibrant and energetic icon was gone, lost forever, and only her memory to linger in our hearts.

I was in constant daily phone contact with my brother, checking on Mom's condition and making sure she was adapting to her new life. I was reassured that despite Mom's advancing age and the level of her dementia, she was doing well. She was comfortable with her surroundings and was not mentally aware of the fact that Hennie and I were not there living with her. I was relieved to know that she was not agitated or upset about not being in her own home, and not disturbed about not seeing me. It saddened me to some degree that Mom had, so to speak, forgotten me; but I had to accept the fact that advancing dementia was the cause. Even though she did not remember me, I remembered her; the mother who was so wonderful and loving to me my whole life. At this point I was glad it was I, not Mom, who was suffering from our separation. All I wanted was for her to be free of anxiety and pain, and to be comfortable, safe, and secure. That was always my goal for her all the years I was taking care of her. It was my duty and my obligation; motivated by love and respect.

Since it was a very short and direct flight to where Mom was, we flew down to see her every few weeks. The first time we went to see her, I was apprehensive as to what to expect. All sorts of horrible images raced through my mind. When we arrived at the nursing home, I was pleasantly surprised to see Mom looking so alert and spry. She was neatly dressed and well groomed. When I leaned down to kiss her, she reacted as if she had seen me every day. She had no clue to the fact that there was any separation or lapse of time since we left her; it was as if she had no sense of time. Hennie and I engaged in conversation with her, but most of the time her words made no sense. She was totally out of touch with reality and her train of thought was very fragmented and convoluted. She still maintained her tender and loving demeanor and her warm gentle smile. As I held her hand, I could feel her affectionate touch as I had always experienced in the past. Even though she was not herself mentally, she was still my beautiful and loving mother physically. Spending time with her in the nursing home was to some extent emotionally fulfilling, but it did not replace the void I felt back home. It was the reality that I had to accept.

On one subsequent visit during that late spring, I noticed that Mom was a little weak and not as spry as she had been in the past. I was not overly concerned and just attributed it to her advancing age. After all, one cannot expect too much energy and exuberance from a ninety-eight-year-old woman. After our visit, we stayed overnight at Tony and Judy's home and planned to return home the next day after seeing Mom in the morning. That morning, we received a phone call from the nursing home informing us that Mom was unresponsive and that her vital signs were very unstable. I authorized them to admit her to the emergency room of the nearby hospital. We all rushed over to the hospital to find out what was wrong with Mom. The doctors informed us that Mom was semi-conscious and suffering from end stage dementia and congestive heart failure. There was nothing they could do except keep her comfortable and partially sedated. My worst fears were now a paralyzing reality, the end was near, and I was powerless to change the course of time.

We took turns that day, staying close to Mom's bed side as she fluctuated between moments of consciousness and sleep. She was mostly unresponsive and only slightly aware of our presence. All we could do was sit with her and hope and pray that she was comfortable and not suffering. There was no improvement in Mom's condition the next day. She was resting comfortably, but her breathing was shallow and labored, indicating that the end was near. Once again, as I sat by her side, my thoughts were filled with all the beautiful memories of our years together as a family. As I held her hand and softly stroked her forehead, I recalled all the times she had lovingly comforted me during my times of pain and sorrow. Even though Mom was not conscious of my presence, I took the opportunity to speak to her in hope that she would hear me. I thanked her for being such a wonderful and devoted mother to me and for all the beautiful years we spent together. I told her how much of a joy it was to be able to have taken care of her during the last years of her life. I told her that I loved her and that I would always keep my love for her in my mind and in my heart. I wanted her to know that she would always be present and alive in me as I carried on the legacy of her values and traditions. I gently kissed her on her forehead in one last tender gesture of affection and love.

A strange sense of calm and peace came over me as I lay down to sleep late that evening after spending an emotionally exhausting day at the hospital. So many thoughts and images kept entering my mind as I drifted off into a deep sleep. I was awakened during the early morning hours by a phone call from the hospital informing me that Mom had quietly and peacefully passed away. I was frozen in time and could only respond with a few short words of acknowledgment. The realization that Mom's life had ended sent a chill through my body; a maternal love, now a void never to be filled, only remembered. I was thankful that she did not suffer and that she was now being protected and loved by God in heaven. I had to quickly suppress my feelings and not dwell on my emotions. It was time to act unafraid and not react emotionally, just as Mom had done so many times in her life. Final arrangements had to be made to insure that Mom's last wishes be respectfully carried out. We contacted the local funeral director and instructed him to conduct an appropriate funeral service and funeral mass for Mom, and to arrange for her body to be transported back to New York to her final resting place next to Dad. It was to be my last loving duty performed for my mother.

The next day, we arrived at the funeral home a few hours prior to the beginning of the wake to have a private family viewing of Mom as she lay in her casket. I knelt down beside her and felt a calm composure grip my body as I stared at her lifeless form. I placed my hand on hers and felt the cold and stiff texture of her skin that was once so warm and tender to the touch. Dealing with the reality of a loved one's death is an emotionally draining event that no matter how hard you try rationalizing it, the heartache and emptiness consumes you. After I said a few prayers over Mom, Hennie came beside me and told me that she thought the way the funeral home had made Mom look was too plain and ordinary. She removed her make-up case from her purse and leaned over Mom and proceeded to add eye shadow to her eyes, blush to her cheeks, red lipstick to her lips, and to redo her hair. Hennie made sure that, even in death, Mom was well groomed and looked her best. It was a tender last gesture that characterized Hennie's love for Mom.

There were very few family members at the wake; my niece, Denise, along with her husband, Rick, and their two young boys, Ashton and Brady, were there. My cousin Johanna flew in from Florida to pay her last respects to her loving aunt. A small group of Tony and Judy's friends from their new neighborhood were also in attendance. A somber aura permeated the softly-lighted chapel. The casket was surrounded by a beautiful array of flowers that cast a regal radiance around Mom. As the people filed by Mom's casket and expressed their condolences to us for our loss, I kept looking at Mom and remarking to myself how beautiful and elegant she looked even in death. I found it extremely difficult to be hospitable to all the people in there while I selfishly sought to be alone and grieve in private. I wanted to quietly savor my last few hours alone with Mom and peacefully reconcile my deep feelings of loss. When it was time to leave, I leaned over and kissed Mom tenderly on her forehead, symbolically wishing her a good night for one last time.

The next morning we viewed Mom's body briefly before having the funeral services at the local Catholic church. It was a beautifully conducted high mass with the choir singing all of Mom's favorite altar music. Denise gave a touching and poignant eulogy that expressed her love for her grandmother and summarized Mom's extraordinary life. Throughout the service, I was overcome with emotion as the finality of Mom's death became a harsh reality. The spirituality of the mass and its message of life after death only vaguely eased my sorrow. I was preoccupied with thoughts of how to deal with my emotions for the next few days and in the future. I realized that I had to focus on the love, joy, and happiness I would be sharing with Hennie by my side in the years to come, and that Mom would always be a beautiful, loving memory to me. After the mass was over, Tony, Judy, Hennie, and I flew back to

New York to await Mom's body that was being flown in later that evening. It was a long, drawn-out day filled with emotion and sorrow for all of us.

The following morning, we had a brief memorial service in the chapel at St. John's cemetery. There was a small gathering of family and friends from the New York area who wished to pay their final and last respects to Mom. My nephew, Anthony, read the eulogy that Denise had so eloquently given the day before. The priest in attendance gave a final prayer and blessing before the burial. Mom would now be in her final resting place in a crypt alongside Dad. After the service concluded, I said my final good-bye to Mom; I placed my hand softly on her closed casket and reluctantly and somberly left the chapel.

We had a luncheon at Dante's restaurant that afternoon for all the people who went to the cemetery for Mom's memorial service. It was not a morose or mournful gathering; it was instead a celebration of Mom's wonderful and beautiful long life. We focused on all the things that made her life so special to each of us individually. There were some tears, but there were mostly smiles and laughter as we all reminisced about our lives with Mom. Her charming demeanor and her fascinating life would always be remembered and talked about by everyone who knew her. Everyone expressed their feelings of loss, but they were comforted by knowing that Mom would always be alive in their hearts and minds. Mom has left us physically, but a part of her lives on in each of us; it is the values and the sense of duty that we witnessed from her exemplary lifestyle that will forever be a part of our lives as we go on in her absence.

It took some time to get used to Mom's absence in our home, but Hennie and I managed to move forward with our lives and share a new beginning filled with love, family, and friends. We continued to have many dinner parties as we had done in the past, and I tried to maintain all the family holiday traditions that were instilled in me my whole life. At the dining room table, where Mom once so prominently occupied her position as hostess and matriarch, now sits my loving and devoted wife, Hennie. She has now taken her place as queen at the head of the table, sharing her love and devotion with family and friends. Every meal, as usual, is an abundant and sumptuous feast enjoyed by all who are invited. As it was once a frequent family tradition to end the meal with a glass of *Strega*, we all now lift our glasses and toast to each other's health in the same fashion as we did when Mom was alive. When I lift my glass of *Strega*, I also silently and lovingly raise my eyes toward heaven and toast to my mother.

TO MOM WITH LOVE... A SON'S STORY

Louise at ninety-six—beautiful and happy

Epilogue

There is no real end to this story; Mom is alive in my mind and in my heart. The values and traditions that she instilled in me by her exemplary life were her legacy to me. The dates of birth and death are the beginning and the end of life, but it is the years in between that are the noteworthy measures that exemplify a person's worth. The summation of the love and caring, and her devotion to family and friends, are what made Mom so special in everyone's life. Taking care of Mom during the final years of her life was the most rewarding and beautiful experience of my life. For me, it was a way of giving back to her all that she had given to me. I wanted to have her live out her life in dignity and comfort with love and respect. Whatever I did for her was immensely rewarding to me internally. My mind and heart are at peace knowing that I had the honor and privilege of being able to shower her with love and devotion. It was my tribute to my mother.

Thank you Mom; I love you!